THE SHOOTING SCRIPT®

THE GOOD SHEPHERD

SCREENPLAY AND COMMENTARY BY
ERIC ROTH

A Newmarket Shooting Script® Series Book

NEWMARKET PRESS • NEW YORK

The Newmarket Shooting Script® Series is a registered trademark of
Newmarket Publishing & Communications Company.

This book is published simultaneously in the United States of America and in Canada.

FIRST EDITION

10 9 8 7 6 5 4 3 2 1

ISBN: 978-1-55704-774-8

Library of Congress Catalog-in-Publication Data available upon request.

QUANTITY PURCHASES

Companies, professional groups, clubs, and other organizations may qualify for special terms when ordering quantities
of this title. For information, write to Special Sales, Newmarket Press, 18 East 48th Street, New York, NY 10017;
call (212) 832-3575 or 1-800-669-3903; FAX (212) 832-3629; or e-mail info@newmarketpress.com.

Website: www.newmarketpress.com

Manufactured in the United States of America.

OTHER BOOKS IN THE NEWMARKET SHOOTING SCRIPT® SERIES INCLUDE:

OTHER NEWMARKET PICTORIAL MOVIEBOOKS AND NEWMARKET INSIDER FILM BOOKS INCLUDE:

*Includes Screenplay

CONTENTS

INTRODUCTION

Since the early 1990s, actor/director/producer Robert De Niro has been researching the subject of what would become his second directorial effort following 1993's acclaimed film *A Bronx Tale*. "Bob has always had an interest in foreign policy and the way that we gather intelligence," relates Tribeca Films and *The Good Shepherd*'s producer Jane Rosenthal.

However, the Academy Award®-winning actor was not interested in directing the standard fare of a spy-game fantasy. He wanted to make a film that would showcase the actual underpinnings of intelligence services and uncover how these largely anonymous men have controlled our world, at both personal and professional costs.

A friend who was aware of De Niro's interest in the CIA introduced him to Milt Bearden, a retired thirty-year veteran of the CIA who would become the lead technical advisor on the film. The former agent, who ran the CIA's operations in Afghanistan in the mid-1980s, agreed to take De Niro across Europe and Asia on an educational journey to explore the hidden realms of intelligence gathering.

From the corners of Afghanistan to the northwest frontier of Pakistan—and off into Moscow—De Niro and Bearden traveled extensively to inform the veracity of what De Niro wanted to explore on film. In his travels with Bearden and in their research together, De Niro became privy to information with which few laypersons are entrusted. "Bob now probably has a better feel for people in the CIA—my generation or the one before—than anybody I've seen that was never in the world itself," notes Bearden.

The author of several books about the CIA, Bearden explains how he is able to share closely guarded details about the United States intelligence operations without sacrifice to the men and women actively serving. "My rule is: 'Don't do anything that hurts anybody or puts anybody in danger, and don't do anything that makes the job harder for anybody who's still trying to do it,'" he shares.

De Niro's continued fascination about intelligence gathering would gestate for several years before he was sent a copy of *The Good Shepherd*—an original script about the early years of the CIA by screenwriter Eric Roth—which dealt with the same issues that were intriguing the director. For the project, De Niro was offered a starring role. Remembers Rosenthal, "Bob immediately said, 'Not only do I want to do this, but I want to direct it.'"

The writer, whose resume includes such popular and critically celebrated works as *Forrest Gump*, *The Insider*, *Ali* and *Munich*, had created a story that wove elements of an exciting spy thriller into the everyday lives of the CIA members who created the agency. "Eric is the best writer working today," Rosenthal compliments. "It was his look at the internal workings of the CIA that we responded to."

Roth was interested in an earlier time period than De Niro had been researching with Bearden, but the two quickly found common ground. "I've been intrigued by the CIA and how it formed," says the writer. "This agency was started with literally seventeen, eighteen people, and has ended up with twenty-nine thousand today."

Framing his story with key events in the CIA's history—beginning the screenplay at the height of the OSS during World War II and closing the timeline with the CIA's failure to accomplish its crucial mission at the Bay of Pigs in 1961—Roth's script examined the lives of the men who formed our nation's modern-day intelligence service.

"I researched people who went into the early years of the CIA and where they came from," Roth says. "It was traditionally Yale and Skull and Bones." Almost exclusively, white male Ivy Leaguers of a patrician class—considered the best and the brightest that the U.S. had to offer—ran the government arm.

In fact, this ultra-secret society counts several prominent Americans as members, including President George W. Bush; his father, former President George Bush (who headed the CIA before becoming president himself); his father's father, Prescott Bush; as well as President Bush's opponent in the 2004 election, John Kerry. "Some were very brave, idealistic people who decided to use it as a public service," adds Roth.

Rosenthal and De Niro responded to Roth's protagonist, Edward Wilson, a sensitive young man who is handpicked to join the OSS in 1939. The producers understood that in telling Wilson's story, Roth was exploring the very personal side of the agency.

"My character, as a young man, was idealistic. There were very good values that I think he was trying to protect…certain things about America that were wonderful," reflects Roth. "He has this good-natured, good-hearted quality of justice. I wanted a character who could help write the rules for how they acted at that point, as he is the heart and soul of the agency.

"I was intrigued with what morals people have and what they're willing to sacrifice," Roth continues. "As I delved into it, I wanted to know more about what kind of lives these guys lived. What was his family life like, and what was life like with his children? What were his dreams for them?"

A certain amount of paranoia would seem not only justified, but inevitable, for the men who headed counterintelligence, but Roth was curious to know where it ended. "I was also interested in this whole psychological effect of entering a world where you don't know what is right or wrong—who your friends or your enemies are," he explains.

Earlier in its history, the United States had had no need for an intelligence organization that mined the depth of foreign information the OSS could provide…until World War II, when our leaders felt it was time for the formation of a covert agency. De Niro offers, "Our country is young at this when compared to Great Britain or other countries that have been doing it a long, long time."

"We had two huge oceans on either side that nobody could do much about," explains Bearden. In Europe, on the other hand, intelligence had been a vital tool throughout the years in creating and maintaining intricate alliances with nearby neighbors. With the end of WWII, however, the U.S. had a new dominant position in the world—and with it, new threats.

"The world became polarized," explains Bearden. "It was the United States and the Soviet Union. You were lined up behind one or the other. And Khrushchev said, 'We will bury you,' and so we said, 'We better figure this out.' After 1945, that was the beginning of the American empire. An American empire without any intelligence capability didn't make any sense."

Roth's Wilson, a product of these polarizing times, sees himself as both America's conscience in dealing with the Soviet Union and as America's protector of freedoms. As head of counterintelligence, his job is to penetrate enemy intelligence and alter our foes' perceptions. He is also charged with learning the internal workings of KGB and what that agency knows about America.

For the filmmakers, the story became an even more important one to tell as all Americans grappled with decisions our government leaders made before the seminal events of September 11, 2001. "I think it was really in the post-September 11 world that people started to pay attention to this subject," reflects Rosenthal. "That's when doors opened, and real discussions began about making this kind of a movie."

More recently, *The Good Shepherd* became even more topical to the filmmakers, with daily headlines about columnist Robert D. Novak's July 2003 outing of Valerie Plame as a CIA operative after an administration source allegedly gave her name. "These are the themes, and this is our subject—this is our national security," Rosenthal adds. "This couldn't be any more current."

In June 2005, Morgan Creek came on board and agreed to produce *The Good Shepherd* with Tribeca. Morgan Creek's CEO, James G. Robinson, recognized Rosenthal and De Niro's passion for the project. He succinctly offers, "This script is as good as it gets."

Robinson was attracted to the story because he felt that it illustrated the similarities both sides share in the Cold War. "I don't think that there was much difference between CIA and KGB," he shares. "The difference is that when the American bureaucracy got out of line, you had remedies to strike back at a system causing harm or discomfort unfairly and illegally. They didn't, obviously, in Russia."

It was important to the filmmakers that the events portrayed in the film ring true to not only audiences, but the architects of American intelligence. Richard Holbrooke, former U.S. Ambassador to the U.N., former Assistant Secretary of State and career diplomat, notes of the film: "*The Good Shepherd* is a fictionalized version of history, which is accurate in almost every incident. But because the filmmakers are liberated from trying to be faithful to the tiny details, they've come a lot closer in many ways to capturing some essential truths about this extraordinary period of intelligence, counter-intelligence, betrayal and espionage during the Cold War."

That is the target for which the filmmakers were aiming. "The film is a mixture of real events and takeoffs of characters," De Niro says. "To be locked into the factual accuracies of those events would be another kind of a movie."

"The Good Shepherd"

Screenplay
by
Eric Roth

2/26/2006   Shooting Script

1   INT. AN APARTMENT   1

A flower arrangement in a VASE on a DRESSER. The sound of
people making love. In the reflection of the dresser MIRROR,
in a darkened BEDROOM, barely distinguishable, a young White
Man and a young Black Woman, on a bed making love. The young
Man's face hidden, lying in her arms, holding him close,
comforting him. We hear sounds of breathing, then a whisper:

                      THE WOMAN
            ...You are safe here with me...

She says something else in his ear we can't hear. He's very
moved by it, and holds her even closer. They whisper. We move
to a nightstand with a lamp and clock reading 10:00. We come
to a wall with chipped paint and an electrical outlet. We go
into outlet to see an iris; it "blinks..." a camera taking a
picture. IN ADJOINING ROOM, A MAN shoots the lovers through
the outlet's holes. A second MAN, smoking, wearing headphones,
monitors a tape-recorder...

2   INT. EDWARD'S SUBURBAN HOME, STUDY - DAWN - APRIL 14, 1961 2

In BLACK, the sound of Wagner's "The Flying Dutchman." Out of
the black, a ship, a "Flying Dutchman," seems to come across
a far horizon... Suddenly a MAN'S HAND, holding a TWEEZER,
comes into frame. Deftly he knots a thread, securing the
mainstay to the mast. He flattens the masts slowly, passing
the ship into the bottle. Our first image of the man is his
reflection, peering into the bottle...

The Man, wearing a bathrobe, at his desk. Wagner's Opera on
RADIO. On a shelf behind Man, a line of ships in bottles...
Just forty, the man is old before his time. Yet there's a
presence here, an intelligence in his eyes, the short but
mussed hair...EDWARD WILSON. He Looks down at his desk at a
grainy BLACK AND WHITE PHOTOGRAPH of a young interracial
COUPLE making love. He switches on a REEL-TO-REEL RECORDER.

SOUNDS of their intimate breathing. The WOMAN'S VOICE again,
"You are safe here with me..." The tape runs out. He rewinds
it. He pushes "Play." He gets up, the sounds of the tape
follow him as he goes down a hall to a bedroom. He begins to
dress, the sound of tape playing down the hall...

3   EXT. 1961, EDWARD'S SUBURBAN STREET, VA - EARLY MORNING   3

A two story red brick COLONIAL on a suburban street. The front
door opens. Edward, in raincoat, with a briefcase, comes out.
He looks around, acutely aware of his surroundings. He locks
the door, takes up a newspaper, and heads down the sidewalk to
the bus stop. Once the Bus comes, Edward lets a man waiting
next to him get on first, then follows...

4   INT. 1961, A CITY BUS, WASHINGTON OUTSKIRTS - EARLY MORNING 4

A Bus filled of men with raincoats, briefcases, newspapers.
Edward, indistinguishable from the rest, has disappeared. We
find him on the aisle by back exit, reading a newspaper, open
to some world news. The Bus stops. People get on and off.

                  A LITTLE BOY'S VOICE (OVER)
        Excuse me.

                                           (CONTINUED)

Edward sees a Woman with a little boy, about to get off bus.

                        THE LITTLE BOY
               Do you have change for a dollar?

Edward looks in his pocket... Takes out some change...

                        EDWARD
               I only have eighty cents.

                        THE WOMAN
                   (Trace of an accent)
               That would be fine, thank you...

They exchange money and the Woman nudges her son to be polite:

                        THE LITTLE BOY
               Thank you, Sir...

                        EDWARD
               My pleasure.

They exit as Edward puts the dollar in his pocket. The bus
pulls off and he slides over to window. He takes up newspaper
and goes to THE PERSONALS. He stops at one: "Dear Mother,
planning a picnic. What's the forecast?" The words reflected
in his glasses...

5   EXT. 1961, STREET, WASHINGTON D.C. - MORNING   5

Edward crosses a street and down some steps into a building...

6   INT. 1961, THE CIA BUILDING, WASHINGTON - MORNING   6

Edward comes down a long empty corridor, a door or two ajar.
A few clerks walk by him, carrying folders with cables to be
delivered to certain offices. He comes to an Outer Office.
Built into the walls are 3 SAFES. Edward turns to a door with
frosted glass that says, "No Exit."

7   INT. 1961, EDWARD'S OFFICE, THE CIA - MORNING   7

Dark, blinds closed, a sparsely furnished, well worn, corner
office. He neatly hangs up raincoat and sits at a desk piled
high with stacks of "Top Secret" CABLES designated "PRIORITY"
and "OPS IMMEDIATE." Edward takes newspaper out of briefcase
and reads The Personals: "Dear Mother, planning a trip, is it
safe to come home?" His secretary enters...

                        SECRETARY
               The other half of the "Split" is on
               your desk.

A Man in his late forties, RAY BROCCO, comes in and puts a
duffel bag on his desk, unzipping it, showing Edward a lot of
money.

                        RAY BROCCO
               From our friends on Wall Street,
               Mother. A two million dollar
               downpayment in our country's
               future...To Miami?

                                                      (CONTINUED)

                         EDWARD
                    Right away.

Ray nods. He starts to go...

                         EDWARD (CONT'D)
                    Mr. Brocco...
                         (going into his briefcase)
                    Somebody left a package on my doorstep
                    last night...

He takes out the reel-to-reel tape and grainy photograph.

                         EDWARD (CONT'D)
                    Have Tech "wash" them right away...

Ray nods, and before he can go...

                         EDWARD (CONT'D)
                    A child asked me this morning if I had
                    change for a dollar.

Ray slows. Edward gives dollar bill to Ray.

                         RAY BROCCO
                    It's from "Cardinal."

Edward blinks, but doesn't say anything.

                         EDWARD
                    Check it.

Ray turns to a safe with color coded files...He opens a file,
looks at the dollar bill, his finger moving down a list of
SERIAL NUMBERS. His finger stops at one. The numbers match.

                         RAY BROCCO
                    Cardinal. He's interested. What did
                    you say, Mother...drop a line in the
                    water you never know what's going to
                    bite...? He bit...

                         EDWARD
                    He's nibbled...Maybe he'll bite...

Edward takes the bill and makes a small DOT on it with a pen.

                         RAY BROCCO
                    I'll have it vapored.

Ray nods and leaves. Edward opens a diplomatic pouch, taking
out a piece of a TRIPLE SPLIT TRANSMISSION. He matches the
zig-zag serrated page with two others to read a message. He
instinctively looks up to see a man with a boyish smile,
standing in the doorway, RICHARD HAYES. He comes over to
Edward's desk, bending down to speak to him.

                         RICHARD HAYES
                    The weatherman says Sunday is a
                    perfect day for a trip to the beach.

Edward looks up and Hayes smiles his "knowing" smile...

(CONTINUED)

                    RICHARD HAYES (CONT'D)
          We're going to stomp that bearded
          little piece of shit into the ground.
          I hope you can still dance, Mother...
          In a couple of days we'll be doing the
          cha-cha in El Commandante's bedroom...

                    EDWARD
               (nods, cold smile)
          I'll have to remember to bring my
          dancing shoes, Richard.

They look at each other, no love lost. Hayes smiles, quickly
turns and leaves. Brocco, everpresent, comes back in.

                    RICHARD HAYES
          Good morning, Ray.

                    RAY BROCCO
          Mr. Hayes.

And Richard leaves...Ray hands Edward two cables...

                    RAY BROCCO (CONT'D)
          Miami...Swan Island. They're ready to
          go. The sooner the better.

                    EDWARD
          Pack a bathing suit, Mr. Brocco. We're
          going for a swim. Tell our friend in
          Miami we're about to set the Mongoose
          free.

                    RAY BROCCO
          It's about time!

And the PHONE RINGS...Ray leaves as Edward picks up.

                    EDWARD
          Yes, Sir. I'll be right up.

8   INT. 1961, THE DIRECTOR'S OFFICE, THE CIA - MORNING   8

A match is lit. A Man, in late sixties, lights a pipe as he
looks out a window... The "Gentleman Spy," PHILIP ALLEN. Edward
stands in the large office. They've known each other for a long
time... Philip flicks a button under his desk, the "Chastity
Belt."

                    PHILIP ALLEN
          The chastity belt is on...I understand
          we're ready to set a fire to our
          neighbors house.

                    EDWARD
          We're day minus two...

                    PHILIP ALLEN
          You must be very pleased. You've
          worked hard on this. It will be
          quite a personal triumph.

                                                        (CONTINUED)

> EDWARD
> You know I don't take anything
> personally, Philip.

> PHILIP ALLEN
> I do. You were always the most serious
> young man I knew. (beat) Toddy and I are
> going to our camp, our mountain house,
> to go fishing. I still have my
> father's, and his father's, fishing rod.

> EDWARD
> (wisely, the axiom:)
> "The first to forget is the last to
> know."

Phillip doesn't say anything. Phone rings. He picks up.

> PHILIP ALLEN
> Yes. Oh? Well, we're just about
> finished, so put it through. (to
> Edward) It's the White House.

> PHILIP ALLEN (CONT'D)
> What do you make of our chances for
> success?

> EDWARD
> If we get the support we've been
> promised I think it's fairly certain.
> If there are any doubts, I can put out
> the fire.

> PHILIP ALLEN
> It's gone beyond that... "Rocking
> chair" is still smiling...

Philip Allen's secretary enters...

> SECRETARY
> It's coming in right now.

> PHILIP ALLEN
> Everybody is waiting for the good
> news, Mother...God speed.

They look at each other, understanding the gravity of the
situation. The meeting over, Allen turns off the radio,
walking Edward halfway to the door...

> PHILIP ALLEN (CONT'D)
> When you're back, come up to the
> mountains and we'll go fishing.

They look at each other a final time...They shake hands and
Edward leaves. Coming through the RECEPTION AREA he can see
in a MIRROR, Philip Allen on the phone. In the mirror's
reflection he "READS" Philip Allen's lips: "Pray to God he
succeeds..." And as Edward leaves...

A9   EXT. 1961, A CAR, THE CARIBBEAN - DAWN - MONDAY, APRIL 17 **A9**

We see Edward looking out the passenger window of a car. Now we see the nondescript car, Ray driving, coming along a rural dirt road, near the water, on a Caribbean island. It comes to an old sugarcane field. It stops outside of a corrugated tin roofed building, "Honduras Sugar Company." "Processing." Edward and Ray get out. Two men silently sitting on a bench outside. Edward and Ray go past them inside...

B9   INT. 1961, CORRUGATED BUILDING, THE CARIBBEAN - DAWN   **B9**

We are inside a Communications Center. Men with headphones monitoring radio reports...A map with colored designations where forces and equipment are. We can hear over the LOUDSPEAKERS radio reports in Spanish from a battle in progress. A Man, standing beside them, oddly whispering, translates for Edward and Ray.

> SPANISH TRANSLATOR
> The brigade is in a critical state. We desperately need air support, two ships have been sunk. More air support now!

> SPANISH TRANSLATOR (CONT'D)
> Enemy on trucks coming from Red Beach are right now 1 KM from Blue Beach...

There are the sounds of the battle from the speakers...Then the voice of a man from the front, in Spanish...

> SPANISH TRANSLATOR (CONT'D)
> 2000 militia attacking Blue Beach from East and West. Need close air support immediately... Can you throw something into this vital point in the battle? Anything? Just let pilots loose.

More fighting...and the Voice in Spanish...

> SPANISH TRANSLATOR (CONT'D)
> Our situation is desperate. We are being attacked by a force armed with mortars, tanks, and T-33 Sea Fury planes. When is help coming?

Edward is quiet. He listens for some more moments...And then we hear the voice from the battle.

> SPANISH TRANSLATOR (CONT'D)
> (translating)
> Am destroying all my equipment and communications. Tanks are in sight. I have nothing left to fight with. Am taking to the woods. I cannot wait for you.

And Edward quietly goes outside...

9   EXT. A REMOTE BEACH IN THE CARIBBEAN - BEFORE DAWN   9

We see Edward standing alone on an empty stretch of
beach...And as Edward looks out across the water...

10   EXT. BAY OF PIGS - DAY   10

We see the aftermath of the Bay of Pigs. And there is CASTRO
WITH HIS TROOPS, LOOKING AT A BOX WITH A COMMANDO'S BODY...
THE BATTLE OVER. STANDING CLOSE BY CASTRO IS A MAN IN HIS
THIRTIES... STAS SIYANKO. Stas walks down the beach to the
water's edge, and looks out across the water...

11   EXT. 1961, THE BEACH IN THE CARIBBEAN - LATER IN THE DAY   11

Edward still standing at the shore, looks out across the
water, while Brocco stands by the car, radio on, the two men
waiting... A distant droning sound. A figure moves quickly
along the beach, a Man in goggles on MOTORCYCLE. He rides up
to Ray, says something, and rides off. Ray crosses to Edward.

                      RAY BROCCO
          The Mongoose is dead... The King still
          wears his crown...

Edward is still. Brocco upset...

                    RAY BROCCO (CONT'D)
          They knew where to find us. There's a
          stranger in our house, Mother...

Edward is silent, watching the waves, rolling onto the
shore, lapping at his feet, one after another...

12PT   EXT. THE MALL, WASHINGTON D.C. - EARLY MORNING   12PT

"THURSDAY, APRIL 20, 1961." The early morning mall empty,
except a figure in the distance. Coming closer, in raincoat,
carrying briefcase, deep in thought, is Edward. He walks pass
the Capitol Building...

12   INT. A DINER , WASHINGTON D.C. - EARLY MORNING   12

"THURSDAY, APRIL 20, 1961." The early morning. Edward walks
into a diner and sees a Man in his fifties, in an old, very
worn fedora, in a booth. Once robust, suit too big now, face
gaunt, a shadow of himself, is SAM MURACH. Edward sits.

                    SAM MURACH
          Somebody on your desk gave the store
          away... told the Soviets where to "find
          you" at the Bay of Pigs... You have a
          mole Mother, very close to home.

Edward doesn't react.

                    SAM MURACH (CONT'D)
          There's going to be an extensive
          "housecleaning" on your side of the
          street...

Edward quietly looks around the diner...

                                             (CONTINUED)

                    SAM MURACH (CONT'D)
          We're not going to be able to do
          business anymore...(a beat) All you
          Yale and prep school boys, you're no
          longer going to be able to run
          things... you thought after Iran,
          Guatemala, you boys were invincible.
          You confused America and all its
          blessings, with being blessed because
          we had you.

Edward doesn't say anything. They're quiet. Two old
warriors. Murach turns his wedding ring around his finger...
bemused...

                    SAM MURACH (CONT'D)
          My ring's even too big...

Edward looks at Murach's hand... the ring a size too big...

                    SAM MURACH (CONT'D)
          Fucking cigarettes. They didn't get
          it all...

                    EDWARD
          I'm sorry.

                    SAM MURACH
          A year, at the most, to live... I
          thought I'd take Carolyn on a trip
          somewhere... I haven't traveled
          much... You've been some places. What
          country would you recommend? I was
          thinking about Spain, maybe...

                    EDWARD
          I don't have any favorites. I was
          always working.

Sam nods. Nothing left to say, he starts to leave, then slows.

                    SAM MURACH
          Be very careful Edward, your name is on
          a "must worry" list...Right on the top.
          And I got enough to worry about...

Edward nods a sincere, "thank you." He looks up at Sam. Sam
nods a fond goodbye, and walks off. Edward notices he's left
his hat in the booth.

                    EDWARD
          You forgot your hat.

As if he didn't need it anymore, he walks off. Edward takes the
hat and runs the brim through his hands, lost in thought. He
slows, feeling something in the brim liner. He takes out a Dry
Cleaners CLAIM TICKET... He gets up, leaving behind the hat...

A13   EXT. 1961, A DRY CLEANERS, WASHINGTON D.C. - MORNING   A13

Edward goes inside a dry cleaners. We can see a Woman at the
counter. He gives her the claim ticket. A moment, and Edward
is handed something, nodding "thank you." He comes out with a
shirt box, wrapped in a pink ribbon.

13   INT. 1961, EDWARD'S OFFICE, THE CIA - MORNING   13

Ray Brocco, gravely concerned, waits for Edward as he walks
toward his office.

                    RAY BROCCO
          Everybody's looking for you.

Brocco reads to him from a phone list:

                    RAY BROCCO (CONT'D)
          ...Mr. Allen called at 03:27 this
          morning, Mr. Hayes called at 03:32...
          General Suarez called from Miami at
          03:37...Stewart from the Post. Mr.
          Allen called again at 03:39...Hadley
          from the Star. Mr. Hayes again at
          03:40...

The Phone Rings, jarring... Ray answers it:

                    RAY BROCCO (CONT'D)
          Survey and Appraisal...(to Edward)
          It's Edward.

                    EDWARD
          I'll speak to Edward first.

Ray doesn't hand the phone over.

                    EDWARD (CONT'D)
          I'll speak to Edward first!

Ray leaves Edward alone...He picks up the phone...

                    EDWARD (CONT'D)
          Where have you been, son? I've been
          trying to reach you.

14   INT. 1961, AN APARTMENT - NIGHT   14

Edward WILSON JR. on the phone. In his twenties, he has his
father's quiet, contemplative nature. The resemblance ends
there. He has a boy's hopeful eyes...

                    EDWARD JR.
          I haven't been staying at the Embassy
          compound. I've been doing some outside
          work. (changing subject) I heard there
          was a setback.

15   INT. 1961, EDWARD'S OFFICE, THE CIA - MORNING   15

                    EDWARD
          Sometimes son, the best laid plans of
          mice and men...I read your message. Is
          there anything I need to know?

16   INT. 1961, THE APARTMENT - NIGHT   16

                    EDWARD JR.
          Everything's fine.

17   INT. 1961, EDWARD'S OFFICE, THE CIA - MORNING   17

                    EDWARD
               (quietly protective)
          Be very careful...

18   INT. 1961, THE APARTMENT - NIGHT   18

                    EDWARD JR.
          I'll be fine. You worry too much. I've
          been very careful, father.
               (the arrogance of youth)
          I have nothing to hide...

19   INT. 1961, EDWARD'S OFFICE, THE CIA - MORNING   19

                    EDWARD
               (quietly)
          Everybody has something to hide.

                    EDWARD JR.
          I have to go. Goodbye.

                    EDWARD
          Please be very careful. Goodbye, son.
          I love you.

We hear Edward Jr. say "Goodnight" as Edward hangs up. He
takes up the SHIRT BOX and opens it. Under two white shirts
are two FILE FOLDERS, FBI FILES on PHILIP ALLEN and RICHARD
HAYES. He unlocks a safe in his desk and locks away the FBI
files. He sits for a moment, then goes to a window darkened by
old wooden blinds. He turns a knob, rotating the slats open.
It's raining. Edward, half in shadow, half in light, lost in
thought. There's a "clank" of a radiator... He looks over as
if he's heard a distant sound... the sound of a KETTLE DRUM...

20   INT. 1939, THE YALE THEATRE CLUB - NIGHT   20

An ORCHESTRA plays in a small COLLEGE THEATRE. On STAGE, a
replica of a quarterdeck of a ship. SAILORS clean brasswork,
splice ropes, performing "H.M.S. PINAFORE.." A roar of
laughter as a buxom redhaired young lass, a large basket of
goodies on her arm, lusty MISS. BUTTERCUP enters, flounces
around the deck, propositioning Sailors, "selling" her wares,
singing in falsetto:

                    BUTTERCUP
          "For I'm called little Buttercup --
          dear little Buttercup.
               (MORE)

                                        (CONTINUED)

20   CONTINUED:

                        BUTTERCUP (CONT'D)
                  Though I could never tell why... But
                  still I'm called 'Buttercup --' poor
                  little Buttercup, sweet little
                  Buttercup, I..."

While she sings, four fair-haired young Men in black suits
come into theatre, standing in shadows by the door... A young
RICHARD HAYES, with briefcase, points out "Miss Buttercup."
He shares a look with a handsome young Man with pale blue
eyes: JOHN RUSSELL.. On STAGE, a BOATSWAIN comes behind Miss.
Buttercup, putting his arms around her waist, fondling her.

                        THE BOATSWAIN
                  "...Aye, Little Buttercup -- and well
                  called -- for you're the rosiest --
                  the roundest -- and the reddest
                  beauty in all Spithead...!"

                        BUTTERCUP
                  "Red, am I? And round and rosy?! May
                  be; for I have disassembled well. But
                  hark ye, my merry friend, hast ever
                  thought that beneath a gay and
                  frivolous exterior there may lurk a
                  canker worm, which is slowly but
                  surely eating its way into one's very
                  heart...!"

She strikes an exaggerated pose as the Orchestra plays on.

21   INT. 1939, DRESSING ROOM, THE YALE THEATRE CLUB - NIGHT   21

Miss Buttercup wipes away makeup at a dressing table as other
cast members change. In the mirror's reflection, the four
young Men in black suits come along a corridor...

                        JOHN RUSSELL
                  Miss Buttercup...

She turns, taking off wig, smiling a pursed lipstick smile...
Miss Buttercup is Edward Wilson at age 20, finely featured
with a boy's smile. Suddenly John firmly clasps his shoulder,
"tapping" him.

                        JOHN RUSSELL (CONT'D)
                  Skull and Bones... Do you accept?

Edward looks at the fair-haired boys. At John. He smiles.

                        EDWARD
                  Accept.

Hayes hands him a rolled document and old book from briefcase.

                        JOHN RUSSELL
                     (Privately)
                  Not a word to anyone, Mr. Wilson. You
                  understand, this is about honor.

                        EDWARD
                  My lips are sealed, sir.

                                              (CONTINUED)

21   CONTINUED: 21

                         RICHARD HAYES
                How does it feel being a woman?

                         EDWARD
                Why would you want to know?

John smiles, liking him. As the young men move off, Edward
watches them go, wiping the lipstick off his ruby red lips...

22   EXT. 1939, YALE CAMPUS - NIGHT   22

We see Edward riding his bicycle coming through the campus...
He comes to "the Tomb", gets off bike, and goes up its steps,
knocking three times with the book on the iron doors.

23   OMITTED   23

24   INT. 1939, A BASEMENT ROOM, THE SKULL AND BONES - NIGHT   24

A darkly lit stone basement, heraldic flags with mystical
Teutonic symbols on walls. Edward, with fourteen other
INITIATES, wear hooded red robes in center of room. BONESMEN,
holding candles, wear hooded black robes, ringing the room...

                         JOHN RUSSELL
                Gentlemen, I will remind you that you
                have taken an oath of secrecy...
                Whatever takes place here is never to
                be repeated to anyone outside of our
                society for the rest of your life...
                The fifteen of you have been chosen to
                be members of America's most select
                secret society. Over a hundred years
                old, Skull and Bones members have
                included a President, Vice Presidents,
                Secretaries of State, Supreme Court
                Justices, Congressmen and Senators,
                captains of science and industry...
                The very best of America...If you
                dishonor us, you will be disinherited,
                as from any family who is
                dishonored...

A door opens, and a Man in a skeleton suit with a crown and
sword enters... While he shuffles, in a "dance of death..."

                         RICHARD HAYES
                     (asks the Initiates)
                Is this the skeleton of a king, a
                nobleman, a beggar or a thief?...The
                character of being a man is all that
                is of importance.

                         THE BONESMEN
                     (intone in ritual German)
                "...Wer war der Thor, wer Weiser, wer
                Bettler oder Kaiser? Ob arm, ob Reich,
                im tode gleich...

                         RICHARD HAYES
                Who was the fool, who was the wise
                man, beggar, or king? Whether poor or
                rich, all is the same in death."

25   INT. 1939, ANOTHER BASEMENT ROOM, SKULL AND BONES - NIGHT 25

Shadowy FIGURES move in a new dance. Focus on young Men, all
naked, laughing. The Bonesmen wrestle with the Initiates in a
room of mud... Edward, locked in a naked embrace with a
Bonesmen on the floor. It's a standoff, neither able to gain
leverage. Hearing something, Edward turns and sees two
Bonesmen and Richard Hayes, laughing, urinating on an
Initiate. Edward suddenly gets up and crosses out of room...

26   INT. 1939, BASEMENT CORRIDOR, THE SKULL AND BONES - NIGHT 26

Edward moves down corridor... John Russell comes out after him.

                    JOHN RUSSELL
          Edward...

                    EDWARD
          I don't think this is for me...

                    JOHN RUSSELL
          It isn't personal... You can't take it
          personally, Edward.

                    EDWARD
          Getting pissed on is personal, Mr.
          Russell... I take it very personally.

                    JOHN RUSSELL
          You're right. It is personal.

They look at each other, covered with sweat and mud.

                    EDWARD
          Is this what they mean by "Bonesmen?"

They both laugh at themselves.

                    JOHN RUSSELL
          We're all in this together, Edward...
          We're brothers...for life.

Edward looks at John with his trustworthy eyes. John puts his
arm around Edward.

                    JOHN RUSSELL (CONT'D)
          Come back inside...

Hesitant, Edward goes back inside with him...

27   INT. 1939, ANOTHER BASEMENT ROOM, SKULL AND BONES - NIGHT 27

A pile of bones. At the apex is an open SARCOPHAGUS Bonesmen
sit semi-circle around. Edward, in robe, stands by sarcophagus.

                    JOHN RUSSELL
          Neophyte Wilson, please remove your
          robe and lie down in the sarcophagus.

He hesitantly starts to take off his robe.

                                             (CONTINUED)

27   CONTINUED: 27

                         JOHN RUSSELL (CONT'D)
                    ...Tell us Mr. Wilson, brother to
                    brother, something you have never told
                    anyone before... Your most guarded
                    secret. Something you will need to
                    trust us with.

Edward is quiet under their gaze, shutting his eyes...

                         EDWARD
                    We had a summer home in Marblehead,
                    Massachusetts...

28   EXT. 1925, THE WILSON HOUSE, MARBLEHEAD - TWILIGHT   28

A July 4th party at a stately home with wide porches, flags
fluttering from stanchions on porch posts, and a large American
flag on a flagpole on a lawn that slopes down to a Bay.

                         EDWARD
                    It was the fourth of July. 1925. I
                    was seven years old...

29   INT. 1939, THE BONES ROOM - NIGHT   29

Edward, lying in the sarcophagus, the Bonesmen around him:

                         EDWARD
                    I went into my parent's room to hide
                    from my friend. I was playing tag with
                    a friend of mine...

A30   INT. 1925, THE WILSON HOUSE, MARBLEHEAD   A30

                         CONNIE WILSON
                    Edward, careful.

                         EDWARD
                    Ok, mother.

Edward, seven, runs up stairs into a bedroom, shutting door.
Another boy comes up...not seeing where he went, he runs off.

30   INT. 1925, THE MASTER BEDROOM, WILSON HOUSE - TWILIGHT 30

Edward hides in his father's closet...Curious, he puts on a
pair of polished Navy dress shoes and walks around, pretending
to be his father. Hearing FOOTSTEPS, he hides back in closet.

31   INT. 1925, CLOSET, MASTER BEDROOM, WILSON HOUSE - NIGHT 31

He huddles among the clothes. Through the slats in the closet,
his father, drink in hand, comes into the room. He sits at his
desk. There are SHIPS IN BOTTLES AND LARGER MODEL SHIPS on a
shelf over his desk. He's still. Methodical, something on his
mind, he writes a note and seals it in an envelope with a
sealer... The clothes hangers click. Hearing this, his father
gets up and opens the closet. Edward looks up at him, afraid.

                         EDWARD
                    I'm sorry I put on your shoes, Father.

                                                      (CONTINUED)

Suddenly, sounds of EXPLOSIONS, fireworks, lighting the room...
His father picks him up, protective, taking him out of closet.
Thomas holds Edward close, talking to him like a little boy:

> THOMAS WILSON
> Have you ever made up a story...told
> your friends something you knew wasn't
> true...? And you know if they found
> out, they wouldn't like you, because
> you lied to them...? Do you know what
> trust is?

Edward shakes 'yes.'

> THOMAS WILSON (CONT'D)
> What is trust?

> EDWARD
> Trust is when you feel safe with
> somebody. Like with my friends. Like
> with you and mother.

> THOMAS WILSON
> That's right...So if you lie to them,
> they won't trust you anymore... and
> you will have nothing. You won't be
> safe. And you'll have no friends. And
> you don't want that, do you?

Edward shakes his head, 'No.'

> THOMAS WILSON (CONT'D)
> Do you understand?

> EDWARD
> Yes, father. I understand. I understand.

> THOMAS WILSON
> That's a good boy. Now go back
> downstairs you're missing the
> fireworks.

He kisses his son, putting him down.

> THOMAS WILSON (CONT'D)
> Tell them I'll be right there... Go
> ahead... go ahead... go ahead...

> EDWARD
> (slows)
> Father, are you coming?

> THOMAS WILSON
> Yes, in a few minutes...go ahead...

Edward looks at his father and leaves the room, going down the
stairs, the fireworks continuing... He decides to go back up,
carefully opening the door, peaking in on his father. His
father raises a pistol to his head, and scared, Edward shuts
the door. A moment, and he hears a pistol SHOT. Edward runs in
to see his father, slumped, pistol in hand, motionless.

(CONTINUED)

CONTINUED: (2)

                              EDWARD
                         (near tears)
                    Father?

Edward is still. He moves towards him, his Father's head on
desk, blood running down the desk, the fireworks sounding. He
sees the envelope... and there are sounds of people running
upstairs... His MOTHER, CONNIE WILSON, and men rush in. Edward
puts the envelope in his pocket. Seeing her husband:

                              CONNIE WILSON
                    Oh my God, no...!

The men run to him... Connie bends to her son... holds him...

                              CONNIE WILSON (CONT'D)
                    What happened? How did it happen?
                    Tell me what happened?!

Edward is paralyzed with fear. His mother holding him...

                              CONNIE WILSON (CONT'D)
                    Ssssssh... it's okay... you didn't do
                    anything wrong... It was an accident
                    wasn't it...?

                              EDWARD
                    I don't know mother I didn't see it.

                              CONNIE WILSON
                         (doesn't hear him)
                    It was an accident... It was just an
                    accident... wasn't it...?

The little Boy nods... whatever his mother says to him...

                              EDWARD
                    It was an accident... It was just an
                    accident, mommy.

And as tears run down his cheeks...

32   INT. 1939, ANOTHER BASEMENT ROOM SKULL AND BONES - NIGHT   32

                              JOHN RUSSELL
                    What did the note say?

                              EDWARD
                    I never read it.

And as Edward lies naked in all respects in the sarcophagus...

33   INT. 1939, A MEETING ROOM, SKULL AND BONES - NIGHT   33

A PHOTOGRAPH OF Edward's FATHER in college. We Pull Back and
see Edward looking at it, along with other class photos in
cases of memorabilia. Bonesmen mingle in a crowded room,
shaking hands with new members... They start to sing Yale's
"The Whiffenpoof Song." Edward watches as Hayes comes over.

                              RICHARD HAYES
                    Congratulations, Mr. Wilson, I'm
                    Richard Hayes, Masters of Secrets and
                    Orders.

He shakes Edward's hand and whispers secretively:

                              RICHARD HAYES (CONT'D)
                    ...That story you told us about your
                    father. Did that really happen?

                              EDWARD
                    Why would I make something like that up?

                              RICHARD HAYES
                    What did the note say?

                              EDWARD
                    I told you, I never read it.

                              RICHARD HAYES
                    You never read the note?

                              EDWARD
                    No.

They look at each other.

                              RICHARD HAYES
                    My father said your father was going
                    to be appointed Secretary of the Navy,
                    until his loyalty was questioned
                    during the war... We're not going to
                    have a problem with your loyalty...?

Edward is silent... Richard smiles his "knowing" smile.

                              RICHARD HAYES (CONT'D)
                    I'm going to be watching you very
                    closely, Mr. Wilson...

And as Edward watches him walk off... the Boys singing...
"Gentlemen off on a spree, gone from here to eternity..."

34   INT. 1939, DR. FREDERICKS' CLASSROOM, YALE - DAY   34

Edward stands in a lecture hall, reading a POEM aloud... John
Russell one of the students. THE PROFESSOR, a tailored man in
early sixties, sits off to side, a cane between his legs,
glasses in hand, eyes closed, listening... DR. WALTER
FREDERICKS.

                              EDWARD
                    That which I know, I know as leaves
                    descending. In dusk, the dark
                    foreshadowed; a stretch of cove, The
                    further thrust of sea's expanse;
                    above, The final solemn promise of our
                    ending.
                              (MORE)

34   CONTINUED: 34

                        EDWARD (CONT'D)
               And yet, a certain word, a glance, a
               guise Will mirror, never show,
               reflecting not My gaze but my
               uncertain question caught Inside a
               shadow of our shifting eyes.

Edward, done reciting, turns, sitting back down.

                        DR. FREDERICKS
               That was quite elegant Mr. Wilson...
               It had good order... Very precise...
               There is a feeling of the unknown...

He has a cultured English accent. Edward, an eager student,
peers out his glasses at him...

                        DR. FREDERICKS (CONT'D)
               Fine poetry is the music of
               mathematics... Numbers singing...
               You have to look behind the words to
               understand their meaning...

BELLS chime the hour. Edward, along with the class gets up...

                        DR. FREDERICKS (CONT'D)
               Good evening...Mr. Wilson... May I have a
               word with you in my office?

                        JOHN RUSSELL
                    (to Edward)
               See you later.

35   INT. 1939, DR. FREDERICKS' OFFICE, YALE - DAY   35

Walking into office...

                        DR. FREDERICKS
               You're very gifted, Edward, a natural
               poet.

                        EDWARD
               Thank you, sir.

                        DR. FREDERICKS
               I'm recommending you as editor for our
               poetry magazine, "The Poeticus."

                        EDWARD
               I'm honored. I appreciate your faith
               in me.

                        DR. FREDERICKS
               Never be ashamed of your talents.

                        EDWARD
                    (nods, noticing)
               Wasn't there a photograph on your
               mantle? A group of men?

                        DR. FREDERICKS
               My father's Crimean War regiment. The
               glass broke. I'm having it fixed.

(CONTINUED)

                         EDWARD
               I remembered seeing it..My father was
               in the war. It reminded me of him.

Under Frederick's briefcase, we see papers under it. One is a
list of names: "The American-German Cultural Committee."

                         DR. FREDERICKS
               You have an acute mind, Edward...You
               are always aware of the smallest of
               details. (smiles, testing him) What
               else has changed in here?

                         EDWARD
               Since I was last here?

                         DR. FREDERICKS
               Yes.

                         EDWARD
               Changed? (a beat, looks) There were
               three umbrellas in the umbrella stand
               last time I was here.

                         DR. FREDERICKS
                    (laughs at his recall)
               I took one home.

He looks around the room and closes his eyes...

                         EDWARD
               I can close my eyes and tell you there
               are at least twelve objects in the
               room that start with the letter "s". A
               sofa. A sugar cube. A stapler. A spare
               shirt. A Spanish book. A sport coat. A
               sink. A suitcase. A scarf. An old
               saxophone. Shakespeare's sonnets. A
               safety pin. That's 12.

Dr. Fredericks laughs. Edward opens his eyes, smiles.

                         EDWARD (CONT'D)
               My father and I, we would play a little
               game. He would ask me to look at a
               room, close my eyes, and tell him how
               many things I could remember with say,
               the letter "T," or "R..." At first, I
               couldn't remember almost anything at
               all. But the more you look, the more
               you see. It's just a game.

                         DR. FREDERICKS
               "Games," can be very real.
                    (after a beat)
               Most people can only see the
               obvious... what's right in front of
               their noses. And sometimes not even
               that.

His eyes meet Edward's. Uncomfortable, Edward looks away...
Dr. Fredericks suddenly turns, looking out a window.

                                              (CONTINUED)

                         DR. FREDERICKS (CONT'D)
              I think we're being watched.

                         EDWARD
              Watched? What do you mean?

                         DR. FREDERICKS
              A man in a hat...

Edward looks out the window.

                         EDWARD
              I don't see anybody.

                         DR. FREDERICKS
              It must be my imagination.

He closes blinds. They find themselves standing close together.

                         DR. FREDERICKS (CONT'D)
              There's so much I'd like to share with
              you, Edward...There's so much I don't
              know about you. I feel like we have a
              kindred spirit...I mean more than a
              particularly bright student...
                         (intimate)
              There's something behind your eyes.

He puts his cane on Edward's shoulder. Uncomfortable, Edward
moves it.

                         EDWARD
              I should be going...

                         DR. FREDERICKS
              I've been trying to write something.
              Would you mind if I read it to you...?

He crosses to his BRIEFCASE... He takes out a small notebook.

                         DR. FREDERICKS (CONT'D)
              "A bud has burst on the upper bough
              The linnet sang in my heart to-day; I
              know where the pale green grasses show
              By a tiny runnel, off the way, And
              the earth is wet. A cuckoo said in my
              brain: "Not yet." It's not finished
              yet.

Edward nods, a flicker in his eyes.

                         EDWARD
              I should be going...

                         DR. FREDERICKS
              I am having some people over to my
              house on Sunday evening. A small
              gathering. I think you might find it
              interesting. Could you perhaps make
              it?

35   CONTINUED: (3)   35

                              EDWARD
                    I'll try to...

As he crosses out of office, Dr. Fredericks points his cane
after Edward, as if he had chosen him for something...

36   INT. 1939, THE YALE LIBRARY - EVENING   36

Edward at library table, intently looking through a POETRY BOOK
by Conrad Aiken. He finds the same poem Dr. Fredericks read to
him. He looks at the library check-out slip, seeing "Dr. Walter
Fredericks" on it. He's quiet, troubled. He studies poem... the
sound of a pencil tapping a table. He looks up and sees a pretty
GIRL studying, unconsciously tapping her pencil, "Connecticut
College For Women" dust jackets on books.

                              EDWARD
                    Excuse me...

Nothing. He softly whistles..."Excuse me." Still no
response...Finally, he stops her pencil from its tapping
altogether...

                              EDWARD (CONT'D)
                    Please...

She starts, looking up. In a small, uncertain voice...

                              LAURA
                    I'm sorry --
                         (motioning)
                    I can't hear...

She smiles, motioning she'll be quiet. They return to their
books. But his interest is in her now. He has a sweet,
vulnerable quality that captures her attention...

                              LAURA (CONT'D)
                    What's your name...?

He smiles, his boyish smile, that's not easy to forget...

                              EDWARD
                    I'm Edward...

                              LAURA
                    I'm sorry. Would you say it again? I
                    have to read your lips.

She closely watches his lips...

                              EDWARD
                    Edward...

                              LAURA
                    Hello Edward... I'm Laura...

                              EDWARD
                    Would you say it again?

She laughs...

                                                        (CONTINUED)

36   CONTINUED: 36

                         EDWARD (CONT'D)
                    Are you writing a paper?

                         LAURA
                    School paper. You?

                         EDWARD
                    Reading some poems.

And as they continue to talk, he crosses to sit beside her...

36A   OMITTED   36A

37   EXT. 1939 YALE CAMPUS - NIGHT   37

Edward comes out of library and crosses to his bike. He passes
right by a fedora lying out there.

                         A MAN'S VOICES
                    ... There isn't one person in a
                    hundred who would just walk by a hat
                    sitting on the ground without giving
                    it a second look...

Edward turns. A heavy-set Man in his thirties, smoking a
cigarette, comes from the shadows behind him. It's SAM Murach,
vital and healthy. He takes up his hat and puts it on.

                         SAM MURACH
                    ...It says a lot about you Mr.
                    Wilson... You aren't easily
                    distracted...
                         (meaning Laura)
                    She's a very pretty girl...

                         EDWARD
                    I don't know you...

                         SAM MURACH
                         (shows badge)
                    I'm Sam Murach... I'm with the Federal
                    Bureau of Investigation...You mind if
                    I walk along with you? I had a chance
                    to have a talk with a fraternity
                    brother of yours, John Russell, the
                    senator's boy... John said you would
                    help us.

                         EDWARD
                    Help you?

                         SAM MURACH
                    You're friendly with Dr. Fredericks...?

Edward realizes Murach was watching him in Fredericks'
office. Edward turns for his bike and sees the front tire is
flat. He mutters a curse and walks his bike. Murach,
uninvited, walks alongside him.

                         EDWARD
                    He's my thesis advisor, if that's what
                    you mean.

                                                          (CONTINUED)

> SAM MURACH
> He's been recruiting faculty members
> and students to join an organization
> called "The American-German Cultural
> Committee." It's a Nazi front... Has
> he talked to you about it?

> EDWARD
> I'm a poetry student, Mr. Murach. I'm
> not political...

> SAM MURACH
> That's not what I asked you. We'd be
> very interested in finding out the
> names of some of the other organizers
> of the "cultural committee..."

> EDWARD
> You want me to spy on Dr. Fredericks?

> SAM MURACH
> "Spying," is what other people do to
> us. I'm just asking you to be a good
> citizen.

And it's quiet. Sam looks around at the campus...

> SAM MURACH (CONT'D)
> You know, I always wanted to go to
> school here... I didn't have the right
> "credentials..." You boys got it made.

He shrugs at life's vagaries, flicking cigarette. Edward starts
to go, then realizes about his tire. He gives Murach a look.

> SAM MURACH (CONT'D)
> If you blow it up it'll be fine...I'll
> be seeing you.

And straightening his hat on his head, Murach walks off...

38   INT. 1939, A MOVIE THEATER, NEW HAVEN - ANOTHER NIGHT   38

Edward and Laura, watching a NEWSREEL, the movie on their faces.

> A MAN'S VOICE
> American Boy Scouts joined their
> German friends at the Boy Scout
> Jamboree in Munich. German Fuhrer
> Adolph Hitler was there to warmly
> greet them...

Reviewing lines of fair-haired young Boys, is Hitler. Mixture
of applause and boos in the theater. Hitler talks with a boy.
The boy says something and Hitler smiles, patting boy's head.

> THE MAN'S VOICE
> A light moment for the German leader.

> LAURA
>   (whispers)
> What are they saying?

(CONTINUED)

> EDWARD
> They're telling us what a good man
> Hitler is.(meaning the movies) You
> sure this is alright with you?

> LAURA
> (shakes "yes")
> I can read Gary Cooper's lips.

LAP DISSOLVE to Laura watching "The Plainsman," reading Gary cooper's lips, saying the words to herself...Edward watches her...she senses this and turns to him. They smile. She slightly flushes and turns back to reading Gary Cooper's lips.

A39   OMIT SCENES A39 AND 39   A39

40   INT. 1939, DR. FREDERICKS' HOUSE - ANOTHER NIGHT   40

A portrait of Hitler on a wall. A group, some Professors and Students, sit in Fredericks' front room, Edward among them...

> DR. FREDERICKS
> We have the privilege tonight of
> having with us, Mr. Haupt, the
> Fuhrer's Education Minister...

A tailored MAN with a swastika on lapel rises to address them.

> THE GERMAN MINISTER
> Good evening. Thank you Dr.
> Fredericks, and members of the
> American-German Cultural Committee for
> giving me the opportunity to come to
> Yale...You will be surprised to know,
> I don't bite.

People laugh.

> THE GERMAN MINISTER (CONT'D)
> It's an honor to be able to speak with
> such esteemed educators and students.
> Germany has always been a country of
> great culture and education...

Edward looks at Dr Fredericks, sitting by a young man. He turns and sees Fredericks' BRIEFCASE on a small table.

41   INT. 1939, DR. FREDERICKS' HOUSE - NIGHT, LATER   41

People mingle over coffee and cake. Edward talks with a Man, eyeing the briefcase. Excusing himself, he crosses the room. He stops, looking at the briefcase, then at Fredericks with the German Minister. Edward, conflicted. After a moment, he walks to briefcase, takes it, and goes into hallway bathroom.

42   INT. 1939, THE BATHROOM, DR. FREDERICKS' HOUSE - NIGHT   42

He sits on the floor, staring at briefcase, folding his arms, upset at betraying his mentor. He opens briefcase. Somebody tries the door. He's motionless... The person leaves. Edward opens briefcase and searches.

(CONTINUED)

42   CONTINUED: 42

He finds a folder -- "American-German Cultural Committee."
Inside, a LIST of names. He takes a pad from his pocket. He
quickly copies names on list, puts list away, and shuts
briefcase. He gets up, opens door, and looks out. The hall
empty. He leaves...

43   INT. 1939, DR. FREDERICKS' HOUSE - NIGHT   43

Edward comes out of the bathroom, making himself some coffee.
He turns and see Fredericks coming towards him... Edward takes
a sip of coffee, revealing that he has somehow managed to
deftly drop off the briefcase in its original place.

                    DR. FREDERICKS
          Edward, how are you enjoying yourself?

                    EDWARD
          Very much.

                    DR. FREDERICKS
          Come, I want to introduce you to Mr.
          Haupt...

44   EXT. 1939, YALE CAMPUS - NIGHT, LATER   44

Edward, hands in pockets, thoughtful, crosses empty quadrangle.
We see Sam Murach, on bench, smoking. Edward puts the copy of
the list on the bench, and Sam puts his hat over it.

                    EDWARD
          Don't ever ask me again.

                    SAM MURACH
          I won't have to...

He walks off as Edward stands in empty quadrangle...

45   INT. 1939, DR. FREDERICKS' CLASSROOM, YALE - DAY   45

Edward sits by John Russell as Dr. Fredericks lectures. BELLS
chime, and Students leave...

                    DR. FREDERICKS
          If you will wait a minute, please...
                (students slow...)
          I have been asked by the Faculty
          Chairman to relinquish my position
          here at Yale. You will hear many
          rumors as to what caused my departure.
          Suffice it to say, I am leaving with
          my name intact.

The Students, quietly talking to one another, leave.

                    DR. FREDERICKS (CONT'D)
          Edward... May I have a moment...

John fraternally taps Edward shoulder, then leaves.

> DR. FREDERICKS (CONT'D)
> What did I do to deserve this? Did you
> have such little regard for me you
> would betray me for my political
> beliefs? Are you that callous?

> EDWARD
> That poem you said you wrote... It
> ends like this..."The last gold bit of
> upland's mown, And most of summer has
> blown away Thro' the garden gate. A
> cuckoo said in my brain: 'Too late.'"
> You know, and I know, Trumbull
> Stickney wrote it in 1929...You were
> my teacher, you betrayed me.

And he leaves the classroom, and a part of himself, behind.
We begin to hear a song playing, "Blue Skies."

46   OMITTED   46

47   INT. 1939, JAZZ CLUB, NEW HAVEN - ANOTHER NIGHT   47

A COMBO plays while a few people dance. Edward and Laura sit at
a table:

> LAURA
> ...I thought we were going to a
> party...?

> EDWARD
> I want you all to myself...

> LAURA
> You want to protect me from them, don't
> you?...You think they will make fun of
> me. I'm not like the girls they see.

> EDWARD
> That's not it...

> LAURA
> It's okay...

She affectionately pushes some hair off his forehead...

> LAURA (CONT'D)
> I'm happy to be with you.

They're quiet. Edward looks at a COUPLE, talking intimately.

> EDWARD
> What are they saying, Laura?

Laura turns, seeing the couple.

> LAURA
> I don't like to "listen" in on other
> people's conversations...

47   CONTINUED: 47

                              EDWARD
                         (innocently)
                    It's alright. They won't ever know.

Laura hesitates, then watching them, reading their lips...

                              LAURA
                         (a beat, slightly flushes)
                    She said she loves him. She said she
                    wants to wait... She wants to be a
                    virgin when she gets married...He must
                    have told her that he loves her...

She can't do it anymore, it's too private. After some moments:

                              EDWARD
                    Would you like to dance, Laura?

                              LAURA
                    I'm not a very good dancer. It's much
                    harder when you can't hear the music.

                              EDWARD
                    That's okay. Neither am I. And
                    besides, I'll lead you.

They get up. He takes her in his arms, "dancing" with
her...Laura follows his lead...

                              LAURA
                    How does this song go?

He SINGS "Blue Skies" to her, so she can hear the words...
She puts her head on his shoulder, comfortable in his arms.

                              EDWARD
                    Would you show me how to lip read,
                    Laura?

                              LAURA
                    Why do you want to learn how to lip
                    read?

                              EDWARD
                    I want to know what it feels like... I
                    want to know everything about you...

                              LAURA
                    You're so serious sometimes...

He smiles, boyish, dispelling her fears. She smiles back...

                              LAURA (CONT'D)
                    Okay. You start with the vowels...
                    Watch my lips closely...

She makes the sound of an "a," forming it with lips... "A,"
"A," "A"... "E," "E," "E"... He watches her lips closely. The
music abruptly stops. The Bandleader makes an announcement.

                                              (CONTINUED)

47   CONTINUED: (2)   47

                    BANDLEADER
          I've just been told England and France
          declared war on Germany. Try to
          continue dancing and enjoying our
          music, and I'll keep you updated as
          info comes in.

It's quiet. Laura notices that people have stopped dancing.
She absorbs the news... The band starts up again, and people
dance, but there's a deep sadness, the end of innocence...
Edward dances with Laura, leading her. They look at each other
intimately. And as much about the world being in chaos...

                    LAURA
                  (awkwardly)
          Before long, we'll be at war too...
          Would you like to get a room for us,
          Edward?

                    EDWARD
          Is that what you want Laura?

                    LAURA
          I think I do.

He looks at her, hesitates, and then turns out of the bar...

A48   INT. 1939, A HOTEL ROOM, NEW HAVEN - NIGHT   A48

Edward and Laura sit on a bed, not quite sure where to begin.
Laura unbuttons her blouse, taking off her bra. They lay back
and kiss awkwardly. It becomes more passionate, his hands
touching her breasts... His fingers catch on a small CROSS on
her neck. He helps her take it off, putting it on top of his
jacket. They kiss some more, becoming more passionate, until
Laura abruptly stops...She sits up. Tears dampen her cheeks.

                    LAURA
          I'm sorry. I thought I could. I can't.
          (putting her clothes back on...) I'd
          like to go home, Edward.

                    EDWARD
          I'll walk you...(seeing that she does
          not understand) I'll walk you.

48   EXT. 1939, A NEW HAVEN STREET - NIGHT   48

Edward and Laura walk by ROW HOUSES. They come to Laura's
porch. An awkward moment, neither wanting the night to end.

                    EDWARD
          Goodnight...

                    LAURA
          Goodnight.

He starts off...

                    LAURA (CONT'D)
          Edward...Thank you.

                                                   (CONTINUED)

CONTINUED:

                         EDWARD
           For what?

                         LAURA
           For being so nice.

Laura smiles... and walks inside. Edward stays on porch,
letting the comfort of Laura linger. A light comes on in
upstairs bedroom. There's movement, Laura getting ready for
bed. As Edward crosses the street, hands in pockets, walking
away, he pulls out Laura's CROSS, inadvertently tucked inside
his jacket pocket. He turns to go back to the house, but sees
Laura's bedroom light turn off. And he walks off...

49   OMITTED   49

50   OMITTED   50

51   EXT. 1940, DEER ISLAND LODGE PORCH - TWILIGHT   51

A large stone LODGE on water, smoke curling from chimney.
People in evening clothes stand on the porch, drinking and
talking. Edward, wearing tuxedo, crosses onto Lodge porch.

                    AN OLDER MAN
           Walker Caswell, Bones 1887.

                         EDWARD
           Edward Wilson, Bones 1940.

He crosses porch, crowded with Skull and Bones Alumni and their
families. He joins John Russell and SENATOR and MRS. JOHN
RUSSELL SR. They talk with PHILIP and TODDY ALLEN, Philip just
starting to gray, smoking his pipe. Toddy, his faceless wife.

                    JOHN RUSSELL
           Edward Wilson, my father and mother.

                         EDWARD
           Senator, Mrs. Russell...

                    SENATOR RUSSELL
           Yes, it's a pleasure to finally meet you.

                    JOHN RUSSELL
           Philip and Toddy Allen... Mr. Allen was
           President of the Bones class of '12.

                    PHILIP ALLEN
           Welcome to our little clubhouse.

A pretty young blonde in an evening gown, holding a drink,
comes to join them.

                    JOHN RUSSELL
           Edward, my sister Clover...

Preppie, she would seem at home in penny loafers, a plaid
skirt and bobby sox. But there's something else in her eyes.
An anger that she doesn't have the courage to be different...
They exchange looks and John introduces them.

                                              (CONTINUED)

51   CONTINUED: 51

                         EDWARD
              Nice to meet you.

                         CLOVER
              Nice to meet you.

The Lodge door opens, a formally dressed Man enters...

                         MAITRE D
              Ladies and gentleman, if you would
              please be seated.

52   INT. 1940, THE LODGE, A DINING ROOM, DEER ISLAND - NIGHT   52

Waiters hurry back and forth. Edward sits with John's family
and the Allen's, Clover across from him. Somebody taps a
glass and the room quiets. An Older Man POUNDS his cane twice
on the floor, and Bonesmen rise and say as one:

                         OLDER BONESMEN
              Bonesmen...

                         BONESMEN
              All here!

They give a rousing SHOUT, and take their seats again...

                         OLDER BONESMEN
              Reverend Collins will offer grace...

                         CLOVER
                  (to Edward, smiles, nasty)
              Bonesmen first, God second...

Edward smiles. They look at each other, attracted.

                         THE REVEREND
              Dear God...

And the patrician heads are bowed...

                         THE REVEREND (CONT'D)
              Thank you for bringing us safely here
              to be with our brothers again...

Edward looks at the bowed heads. His eyes meet RICHARD HAYES'
across room. He smiles with a look of unfinished business. As
the room prays, Edward looks at all the "People like us."

                         THE REVEREND (CONT'D)
              ...We thank you for guiding the Evans
              Family Trust in the care of our island,
              so that we may come here and be with our
              families and friends in comfort and
              privacy...
                         (MORE)

52   CONTINUED: 52

                    THE REVEREND (CONT'D)
              We thank you Lord, for giving us our
              privileged place on this good earth, for
              letting us taste the sweet fruit of your
              bounties...We come here, Lord, in
              uncertain times, and we ask that you give
              us the counsel and the strength to help
              guide our ship of state through the
              turbulent waters...In the name of God,
              Amen.

                         CLOVER
              Well. That was fun.

53   INT. 1940, THE LODGE, DEER ISLAND - NIGHT   53

Tables pushed aside, people dance as A BIG BAND plays with a
well known CROONER. Edward quietly stands watching...

                    CLOVER'S VOICE
              Don't you dance, Mr. Wilson?

He turns, and Clover, holding a drink, comes over to him.

                         EDWARD
              Nobody asked me.

                         CLOVER
              I think I'll take my chances... I'm
              asking...

Glass in hand, she walks him to dance floor. While dancing:

                    CLOVER (CONT'D)
              John is very fond of you.

                         EDWARD
              I'm very fond of him too.

                         CLOVER
              He's talking of going to fight with
              the English. My father isn't
              particularly pleased about it. He's
              one of the organizers of "America
              First." It wouldn't look very good for
              an isolationist's son to go off to
              war, would it?

                         EDWARD
              John's a man of great conviction. I
              admire him.

                         CLOVER
              What about you, Mr. Wilson? What do
              you believe in?

Edward doesn't say anything. After some moments:

                         EDWARD
              Are you in school?

                         CLOVER
              I'm finishing at Wellesley.

53   CONTINUED: 53

Edward nods, and he's quiet again.

                    CLOVER (CONT'D)
            You don't have much to say, do you,
            Mr. Edward Wilson...?

                    EDWARD
                (his smile)
            When there's something worth saying.

She laughs at his arrogance.

                    CLOVER
            You seem pretty sure of yourself Mr.
            Wilson.

                    EDWARD
            I know what I know.

                    CLOVER
            I think I'm going to like you...

She brazenly puts her arms around his neck, dancing. They
look at each other, attracted... Senator Russell comes over:

                    SENATOR RUSSELL
            Excuse me, dear...
                (to Edward, discreet)
            Could I have a moment...?

                    EDWARD
            Will you excuse me...?

She raises her glass to him, nodding... smiles, knowing...

                    CLOVER
            Nasty little secrets.

Edward follows the Senator to a far corner. The Senator talks
with Edward as Philip Allen comes over and says some words.
Edward nods and leaves with Philip Allen.

54   EXT. 1940, BILL SULLIVAN'S CABIN, DEER ISLAND - NIGHT   54

Edward and Allen cross to a CABIN by the water. An Army Man
stands guard outside. RICHARD HAYES comes out of the cabin.

                    PHILIP ALLEN
            Mr. Hayes...

                    RICHARD HAYES
            Gentlemen...

He walks off. The Guard shows them inside...

55   INT. 1940, BILL SULLIVAN'S CABIN, DEER ISLAND - NIGHT   55

A dark haired Man in his late fifties, overweight, with the
face of a drinker, GENERAL WILLIAM SULLIVAN, on a couch,
briefcase by side, his shoes and socks off, feet by a fire...

                                                    (CONTINUED)

55   CONTINUED:

> PHILIP ALLEN
> General William Sullivan, Mr. Edward
> Wilson.

> EDWARD
> It's a great honor, sir.

> BILL SULLIVAN
> I'd get up and shake your hand but my
> fucking feet are swollen... Something
> about too much sugar in my blood and
> my urine... Thank you, Philip -- I'm
> sorry to disturb your weekend...

> PHILIP ALLEN
> It's not a problem.

> BILL SULLIVAN
> When do you boys start your pissing
> contests?

Philip Allen laughs.

> PHILIP ALLEN
> I'll excuse myself...

He discreetly leaves... It's quiet.

> BILL SULLIVAN
> Sit down if you want...

Edward doesn't.

> EDWARD
> If you don't mind, I'll stand sir.

> BILL SULLIVAN
> No, sit down, please, I'd appreciate
> it. I knew your father from the "Great
> War." I was on a ship he commanded in
> the North Sea. It was as close as I got
> to seeing Ireland... Your father was a
> cold son of a bitch... but smart. Smart
> as they come. He was a great Navy man.
> A great American. He would have done
> even greater things for our country. I
> never believed a word of the
> accusations against him. I miss him.

> EDWARD
> So do I.

It's quiet.

> BILL SULLIVAN
> I'd appreciate if you'd sit down. I
> don't really want to have to look up
> at you.

Edward sits down.

(CONTINUED)

> BILL SULLIVAN (CONT'D)
> You understand whatever we discuss
> here doesn't leave this room...?

> EDWARD
> Of course.

> BILL SULLIVAN
> People tell me you're exceptionally
> bright... that you're an honorable and
> trustworthy man... and that you love
> your country...

> EDWARD
> I love my country very much, sir.

> BILL SULLIVAN
> We will eventually get involved in
> this war. Not because we want to, but
> because we have to... And we should...
> The President has asked me to look
> into creating a Foreign Intelligence
> Service... If it happens, I'll be
> looking for patriotic, honorable,
> bright young men, from the right
> backgrounds, to manage the various
> departments. In other words, no Jews
> or Negroes, and very few Catholics...
> And that's only because I'm a
> Catholic... You'll be trained and
> commissioned in the army, and posted
> overseas... If it's something that
> interests you, you'll have to be ready
> to leave at a moment's notice... I
> don't want your answer now -- think
> about it... But this isn't a bunch of
> fraternity boys sitting around playing
> with their pricks... This is for real.
> For America.

A KNOCK, and the Guard says, "It's time General." The General
puts his socks back on, struggling...

> BILL SULLIVAN (CONT'D)
>   (putting shoes on)
> Do you have a personal item you can
> give me? A pin, a pen, something only
> recognizable as belonging to you.

Not quite understanding, Edward takes out his wallet and gives
him Laura's CROSS. The General pockets it and hefts his big
body up, and shakes Edward's hand...

> BILL SULLIVAN (CONT'D)
> We never met, and we never had this
> conversation.

A56   EXT. 1940, A DOCK, DEER ISLAND - NIGHT   A56

General Sullivan boards a motor launch with his Aide, and the
boat pulls away, into the distance...

EXT. 1940, A COVE, DEER ISLAND - NIGHT

Edward and Clover sit by a fire with John and a young blonde
in an empty cove, passing a flask, all a bit drunk. John and
the young Girl are all over each other. Taking a blanket and
smiling at Edward, John walks off with her. Clover, drunk and
pissed off at the world...

                    CLOVER
          I'm supposed to be looking for the
          perfect husband. Are you the perfect
          husband, Mr. Wilson?

                    EDWARD
          Perfect in every way.

She laughs...They're quiet...After a beat:

                    CLOVER
          Is there some reason you won't put
          your arm around me...?

Edward awkwardly puts his arm around her. She lays her head
on his shoulder, the orchestra playing in the distance.

                    CLOVER (CONT'D)
               (sings, sarcastic)
          "...Night and day you are the one.
          Only you beneath the moon and under
          the sun..."

Clover suddenly kisses him. Edward, conflicted, pulls away.

                    CLOVER (CONT'D)
          Do you have a problem with women, Mr.
          Bones...?

He's quiet. She looks at his boy's eyes, and suddenly pushes
him down, roughly kissing him. Her hand fumbles for his belt,
unbuckling it. She reaches, clasping him. Edward responds and
kisses her hard. They roll on the ground, passionately
kissing. She lifts her dress and lets him get on top... He
fumbles to enter her... she stops him...

                    CLOVER (CONT'D)
          Do you love me?

                    EDWARD
          What?

                    CLOVER
          Tell me you love me.

He can't. But he can't stop either. She whispers in his ear:

                    CLOVER (CONT'D)
          Tell me you love me... tell me you
          love me... tell me you love me...

And Edward, compromised, to where he will say anything...

(CONTINUED)

56   CONTINUED: 56

                              EDWARD
                          (quietly)
                    I love you.

                              CLOVER
                    I don't believe you...

                              EDWARD
                          (in the throes of passion)
                    I do... I think I love you... I love
                    you...

She sighs and lets him inside her as they make love by fire...

57   OMITTED   57

A58   OMIITED   A58

58   EXT. 1940, THE CONNECTICUT SHORE - DAY   58

Edward and Laura sit on a blanket in tall grass in sand dunes,
on a date at the beach.

                              LAURA
                    I'm going to save my money...As soon
                    as the world comes to its senses, I'm
                    going to travel...To London and Paris
                    and Rome...Istanbul...Bombay...
                    Jerusalem. Don't you want to see the
                    world, Edward. You could come with me.

Sensing their vast differences:

                              LAURA (CONT'D)
                    We're worlds apart...

                              EDWARD
                    What do you mean?

                              LAURA
                    We come from two different worlds.

                              EDWARD
                    Why do you say that, Laura?

                              LAURA
                    Sometimes, I feel like I'm just a
                    curiosity to you... I'm not real to
                    you...I don't belong...

                              EDWARD
                    That's not true... That's not true at
                    all... That's not how I feel about you.

He looks at her. Needing to show his feelings are real, he
kisses her, hungry, like it's the last time. Edward, feeling
a shadow, turns. A CAR'S come to a stop above the dunes. JOHN
RUSSELL gets out, calling out for Edward. Something's
wrong... Edward crosses to him.

                              EDWARD (CONT'D)
                    John...?

                                                          (CONTINUED)

58   CONTINUED:

                        JOHN RUSSELL
                I've been looking everywhere for
                you... (beat) Edward, my sister...

We see Laura's watching them... reading John's lips...

                        JOHN RUSSELL (CONT'D)
                She's pregnant, Edward...

The implications are obvious. Edward, remembering Laura can
read their lips, moves to stand between her and John...

                        JOHN RUSSELL (CONT'D)
                I know you will do what's expected of
                you... You are an honorable man...

The words resonate. Edward turns and sees Laura's gone off,
walking away down the beach. He puts his hands in his pockets
and turns to John.

                        JOHN RUSSELL (CONT'D)
                You love her, don't you?

And he embraces Edward like a brother.

                        A REVEREND'S VOICE (OVER)
                ...Do you Edward Bell Wilson...

59   EXT. 1940, AN EPISCOPALIAN CHURCH, CT - DAY   59

An old New England CHURCH. We hear a reverend's voice over:

                        THE REVEREND (OVER)
                ...Wilt thou have this woman to be thy
                wedded wife, to live together after
                God's ordinance in the holy estate of
                Matrimony? Wilt thou love her,
                comfort, honour, and keep her in
                sickness and in health; and, forsaking
                all others, keep thee only unto you,
                so long as ye both shall live?

                        EDWARD'S VOICE
                I do.

60   INT. 1940, THE RUSSELL ESTATE, GREENWICH, CT - DAY   60

Edward cuts the cake, feeding a piece to Clover. People
laugh, applaud, then move around the wedding reception,
eating and drinking. The Bonesmen gathered together,
laughing, talking. Clover with her Wellesley sisters. Edward
quietly talks with his Mother, who has the gray pallid look
of an alcoholic. John comes over and discreetly tells him...

                        JOHN RUSSELL
                There's a man in a uniform here to see
                you.

Edward goes to the door. An Army Man waits in the foyer.

                        THE MAN
                Mr. Edward Wilson?

                                                    (CONTINUED)

Edward nods.

                    THE MAN (CONT'D)
          If we could speak alone, sir.

Edward follows him to another room.

                    EDWARD
          Would you like to sit down?

                    THE MAN
          No thank you, sir.

                    THE MAN (CONT'D)
          General Sullivan sends his regards.

He gives Edward back Laura's CROSS.

                    THE MAN (CONT'D)
          I'm to ask you, if you are still
          interested in seeing the rest of the
          world?

Edward looks at the cross in his hand. He looks at the house,
the people, all it entails... A chance to serve his country.

                    EDWARD
          Yes sir, I certainly would.

The Man gives him an envelope with orders, salutes, and
leaves in a car. Edward, excited, looks at his orders. He
instinctively turns. He sees Clover nearby, looking at him.

                    EDWARD (CONT'D)
          I've got my orders. I'm going
          overseas.

                    CLOVER
                (slowing)
          When?

                    EDWARD
          One week. I'm to report to Camp X
          For a ten week training course.

                    CLOVER
                (fingering her bodice)
          What are you going to do, Edward?
          Save the world?

After a few moments...

                    EDWARD
          I'll do what I can.

She looks at him and suddenly embraces him, understanding like
so many women did during the war, that she must suffer alone.

                    CLOVER
          Well, at least we'll have time for a
          "Honeymoon."

                                                      (CONTINUED)

60   CONTINUED: (2)   60

A moment and she turns back to the party, leaving Edward by the
open door, still just a boy really, ready to save the world.

61   INT. 1961, A TECHNICAL ROOM, THE CIA BASEMENT - DAY   61

"Friday, April 21st, 1961." Light and shadows... PULL BACK
and see a BLOW-UP of a grainy BLACK AND WHITE PHOTOGRAPH of
INTER-RACIAL COUPLE on wall. Edward, Ray Brocco, and three
CIA OFFICERS in a Technical Room. The REEL-TO-REEL TAPE over
SPEAKERS play SOUNDS OF INTIMATE BREATHING, the Woman's
VOICE: "You are safe here with me..."

Another Technical Officer stands by the BLOW-UP of the
original photograph.

                    TECHNICAL OFFICER # 2
               ...We're having problems pushing the
               size of this much further... the
               resolution breaks down pretty
               quickly... the film stock is
               definitely Russian, low-grade...The
               photograph is particularly dark. We
               can see a Caucasian man and a Negro
               woman.

                    TECHNICAL OFFICER # 1
               Assuming we're talking about the same
               women...The linguists tell us her
               accent is Francophone...possibly
               French African.....

                    EDWARD
               In how many countries in Africa is
               French spoken?

                    TECHNICAL OFFICER # 1
               Ten countries... millions of people...
               It would do us no good if there
               weren't some other indicators...

                    TECHNICAL OFFICER # 2
               One of the areas we've been focusing
               on is the mosquito netting. Mosquito
               netting is predominantly in Africa,
               Southeast Asia, any tropical
               climate... And the window curtains
               here... They have a definite pattern
               on them... Of trees.

He points to a distinctive pattern on the WINDOW'S CURTAINS,
then passes an 8 x 10 BLOW UP to Edward.

                    EDWARD
               What kind of trees are they?

                    TECHNICAL OFFICER # 2
               We're told by our experts they are
               Baobab trees...

                    EDWARD
               What are they native to?

                                                    (CONTINUED)

                              TECHNICAL OFFICER # 2
                    Africa, Madagascar, and Northern
                    Australia... Next to the curtains,
                    there's a balustrade with a pigeon
                    here. The balustrade appears to be
                    chipped. We're told by our experts
                    that the material of the building
                    makes it at least fifty years old or
                    older...

                              TECHNICAL OFFICER # 1
                    Outside the apartment, if you listen
                    closely, you can hear an airplane...
                    We've washed it out...

          He plays the SOUND of an AIRPLANE...

                              TECHNICAL OFFICER # 1 (CONT'D)
                    ...By the sound of the thrust of the
                    jet engines we can determine it's a
                    plane taking off... no more than a
                    thousand feet off the ground...

                              Edward
                    How far out is that?

                              TECHNICAL OFFICER # 1
                    Two miles out... Wherever this was
                    recorded is no more than two miles
                    from an airport... A jet would limit
                    it to a major city's airport... We
                    also have some car horns...

          He plays the sound of CARS' HORNS...

                              TECHNICAL OFFICER # 1 (CONT'D)
                    There is nothing particularly
                    remarkable about the cars' horns...
                    The cars are of either European or
                    American origin... but this one we
                    were able to separate...

          He plays a particular CAR HORN...

                              TECHNICAL OFFICER # 1(CONT'D)
                    Our experts tell us it's a Russian
                    "Volga's" horn... It's the only car's
                    horn that sounds like a large fart...
                         (a beat)
                    We're still analyzing it...There are
                    also church bells.

          He plays the sound of the CHURCH BELLs...

                              TECHNICAL OFFICER # 1(CONT'D)
                    There are three bells. Two smaller.
                    One larger--they play at five second
                    intervals. Church bells are almost
                    exclusively used by Christian
                    faiths... The volume indicates that
                    the church is no more than a block
                    away. Maybe less.
                              (MORE)

61   CONTINUED: (2)

                        TECHNICAL OFFICER # 1(CONT'D)
                   And the timbre of the bells' ring
                   suggests they're quite old...

                        EDWARD
                   How old?

                        TECHNICAL OFFICER # 1
                   At least a hundred years old...
                   Perhaps it's in an older area of a
                   city...?

Click to a slide of the church's steeple.

                        TECHNICAL OFFICER # 2
                   We can see in a makeup table's mirror,
                   the reflection out a window...a
                   church's steeple..

He clicks to a shot of the nightstand.

                        TECHNICAL OFFICER # 2 (CONT'D)
                   On The night stand here, we can see a
                   clock. It reads almost 10:00...Which
                   could correspond to the church
                   bells...

He shows them the CLOCK, the frozen hands of time...And he
plays the sound of a ceiling fan turning.

                        TECHNICAL OFFICER # 1
                   I've got audio of a ceiling fan. It's
                   a Four-blade, standard ceiling fan. We
                   don't know where it's from.

The projector clicks to a shot of a standing fan:

                        TECHNICAL OFFICER # 2
                   There's a   standing fan over here...
                        (showing them)
                   We can't quite make out the brand
                   plate yet...It could help in
                   identifying the location...

                        TECHNICAL OFFICER # 1
                   But from what we've been able to
                   determine so far, the tape's from a
                   major city with Russian contacts... A
                   place that's either tropical or in
                   their summer season -- the ceiling fan.
                   Close to a major airport... And French
                   is either spoken there, or the voice is
                   a visitor's who speaks French...

                        TECHNICAL OFFICER # 2
                   There's also something here...

We see an indistinct OBJECT on the night stand...

                        TECHNICAL OFFICER # 2 (CONT'D)
                   It could be nothing significant...
                   maybe a candle, a paper weight... or,
                   maybe it's something personal that
                   will help us identify the people in
                   the room...
                        (MORE)   (CONTINUED)

61   CONTINUED: (3)   61
                              TECHNICAL OFFICER # 2 (CONT'D)
                         We're going to wash it again, maybe we
                         can see what's there...?

Edward gets up and peers through his glasses at the blow-up
of the indistinct reflection. The recording is playing, the
WOMAN'S VOICE, "You are safe here with me..." He slightly
blinks at a thought...

                              EDWARD
                         How long until we can get some
                         definition on where this exactly is.

                              TECHNICAL OFFICER # 2
                         We're going as quickly as we can, sir.

Edward looks down into the wilderness of light and shadows...
There's the sound of a small BELL RINGING...

62   EXT. 1941, TAILOR SHOP, LONDON - DAY   62

Edward outside a small London TAILOR SHOP, wearing an overcoat.
A tailored Man opens the door, and Edward goes inside.

63   INT. 1941, TAILOR SHOP, LONDON - DAY   63

                              THE MAN
                         Good evening. May I help you sir?

                              EDWARD
                         I would like to see a tailor about a
                         fitting for a new suit.

                              THE MAN
                         What kind of suit are you interested
                         in sir? Would that be tweed? Worsted?
                         Gabardine?

                              EDWARD
                         Worsted. And a tweed.

                              THE MAN
                         Both single breasted?

                              EDWARD
                         Yes.

                              THE MAN
                         Two or three buttons?

                              EDWARD
                         Three buttons.

                              THE MAN
                         If you might come this way, sir...

He follows man into a room with three MALE TAILORS on
machines sewing. The Man parts curtains:

                              THE MAN (CONT'D)
                         Please... Our senior tailor will be
                         right with you, sir...

64   INT. 1941 DRESSING ROOM AREA, TAILOR SHOP, LONDON - DAY   64

Edward goes into dressing room area and the Man closes the
curtain. A few moments, and Edward goes into a private
dressing room, waiting... The curtain soon parts. Pipe in
hand, is PHILIP ALLEN. He shuts the curtain...

                  PHILIP ALLEN
        Welcome to London...It's nice to see
        you again, Edward...

                  EDWARD
        Nice to see you, sir.

                  PHILIP ALLEN
        I understand you recently were
        married... Congratulations...

                  EDWARD
          (shakes hands)
        Thank you...

Philip motions. They sit on a bench and Allen lights his pipe.

                  PHILIP ALLEN
        You are going to have to learn as
        quickly, and thoroughly as possible,
        the English system of Intelligence...
        The black arts... particularly
        counterintelligence, the uses of
        disinformation, information and how
        its used is ultimately power...

Edward is quiet.

                  PHILIP ALLEN (CONT'D)
        They've agreed to open up their
        "operations" to us -- they can't win
        the war without us - but they don't
        really want us here... Intelligence
        is their mother's milk, and they don't
        like sharing the Royal Tit with people
        who don't have titles.

He draws on his pipe. After some moments:

                  PHILIP ALLEN (CONT'D)
        I'm going to be working out of
        Switzerland -- I still have some
        business relationships in Germany that
        can be useful...

Edward nods. He gets up to go.

                  PHILIP ALLEN (CONT'D)
        There will be very few people in the
        intelligence community you can
        trust...For the sake of your sanity
        you will need to trust someone...That
        someone will be me. Your London tutor
        is ready to meet you. God speed.

(CONTINUED)

They look at each other. Philip offers his hand. They shake.
Philip opens the curtains and motions at a door into another
ROOM: Edward goes down through the door and is led by a
Security Officer.

                    SECURITY OFFICER
          This way, sir.

Edward enters a small COMMUNICATIONS ROOM with a few Short
Wave Radio Stations and Communication Officers with
headphones, receiving and transmitting messages. In the
background, we hear a Woman reading numbers in a monotone:
1...3...7...8...

                    A MAN'S VOICE (OVER)
          I should have known better than to use
          Stickney.

Edward turns. He stops, startled. It's DR. FREDERICKS, leaning
on his cane, standing under a sign, "Silence is Golden."

                    DR. FREDERICKS
          Job well done, Mr. Wilson. You blew a
          two year operation for me. I told
          General Sullivan to keep an eye on
          you. (beat) Just as well. I was
          starting to long for the bone chilling
          cold of home...

He affectionately offers his hand.

                    DR. FREDERICKS (CONT'D)
          It's good to have you in London,
          Edward.

                    EDWARD
               (adjusting, impressed)
          It's good to be here, sir.

                    DR. FREDERICKS
          It isn't personal.

Edward looks around, a secret world at work...

                    DR. FREDERICKS (CONT'D)
          It's like watching someone in their
          bedroom when they don't know you are
          there.

65   INT. 1941, LONDON PUB - NIGHT   65

Edward and Dr. Fredericks at a corner table at a pub...

                    DR. FREDERICKS
          ...Learn your "tradecraft" well...
          particularly the use of "black
          propaganda" -- and the ingredient
          known as "playback," understanding how
          effectively your own disinformation is
          actually working on the enemy...

65   CONTINUED: 65

       And there's the ominous sound of an AIR RAID SIREN...
       Fredericks grabs two glasses and a liquor bottle...

                        DR. FREDERICKS (CONT'D)
                   Drink up, Edward. Alright, off we go.

A66   OMITTED   A66

B66   EXT. THE LONDON TUBE - NIGHT   B66

       As Edward and Fredericks enter a Tube Station...

                        DR. FREDERICKS
                   It's vital to penetrate the enemy's
                   intelligence services in order to push
                   the enemy into an unreal world... "a
                   wilderness of mirrors," as it were...

66   INT. 1941, THE LONDON TUBE - NIGHT   66

       Distant sounds of the Blitz as Edward and Fredericks walk
       through station and down the endless ramp to the tracks...

                        DR. FREDERICKS
                   The very qualities that make a good
                   intelligence officer...A suspicious
                   mind, the love of complexity and
                   detail, an ability to detect
                   conspiracies...are also the qualities
                   most likely to corrode natural
                   intelligence and objective
                   judgement... you see only what you
                   want to see... The danger, Edward, is
                   that you become obsessed with somebody
                   or something that is crawling around
                   inside your head...And you shut
                   everything else out, and only listen
                   to what's going on inside your own
                   head. Anybody that puts up the
                   contrary side, you see, is guilty of
                   sinning against your own special Holy
                   Ghost...

       Fredericks looks through the empty glass in his hand.

                        DR. FREDERICKS (CONT'D)
                   ...It's like looking through an empty
                   glass. Everything that seemed clear is
                   bent, everything that seemed bent is
                   clear... Through a glass darkly...
                   Here we are...

       They come to 2 empty cots, a subway alcove, lights flickering,
       as hundreds of Londoners hunker down for the night.

                        DR. FREDERICKS (CONT'D)
                   Hello all...Cheers...

       The people on the other cots all seem to know him...

                        DR. FREDERICKS (CONT'D)
                   You get very chummy down here...

                                                    (CONTINUED)

He sits on a cot...He motions Edward to sit on a cot next to
his...There's the constant distant rumble of the bombs...Dr.
Fredericks takes out the glasses and pours them a drink...

                    EDWARD
          By that logic, how do I know if I can
          even trust you?

Dr. Fredericks takes another drink...and his final admonition:

                    DR. FREDERICKS
          You won't. I hope you find someone to
          trust. I'm sorry to say, I haven't.

And the lights flicker and suddenly go out altogether...The
endless people in silence in the dark tube...He lays down
putting a blanket around himself...Edward lays down, pulling
a blanket up. And Fredericks starts to sing an old English
ditty as the world falls on top of them...

67   INT. 1941 EDWARD'S O.S.S. OFFICE OLD LONDON BUILDING - DAY 67

Edward sits at desk reading a report. A knock. RAY BRACCO, in
early thirties in an Army uniform and greatcoat enters.

                    RAY BROCCO
          Mr. Carlson?

Edward doesn't look up, reading.

                    RAY BROCCO (CONT'D)
          Is this the American Trade Bureau?

                    EDWARD
          Which product?

                    RAY BROCCO
          Dry goods.

                    EDWARD
              (still not looking up)
          You're late.

                    RAY BROCCO
          Yeah, that's what my mother said.

Edward tries not to smile. He reads aloud from the report...

                    EDWARD
          ...Raymond Duca Brocco, born May, 8,
          1907, New York City...St. Ignatius
          High School... Fordham University...
          married to Anita Delvecchio...
          Children, Carolyn and Steven... six
          and eight... Height 6'2, weight 182
          lbs. Black hair. Brown eyes...
          military service...

He looks through some official army records...

                                                    (CONTINUED)

                       EDWARD (CONT'D)
        Five years military intelligence.

He reads to himself. He looks up for the first time...

                       EDWARD (CONT'D)
        Is there anything you want to add?

                       RAY BROCCO
        My children's names are Stephanie and
        David.

                       EDWARD
        I know. I wanted to make sure you did.

                       RAY BROCCO
        Do you want to look up my ass, too?

                       EDWARD
        You're working for me, Sergeant Brocco.

                       RAY BROCCO
        I'm working for the United States
        Government, sir.

                       EDWARD
        In this office, I am the United States
        Government...

                       RAY BROCCO
        You're pretty sure of yourself for
        somebody who just began.

Edward doesn't say anything. After a beat:

                       RAY BROCCO (CONT'D)
        They wouldn't tell me your name.

                       EDWARD
        Then how do you know you aren't in the
        wrong place?

                       RAY BROCCO
        They said you were a serious S.O.B
        that didn't have any sense of humor.
        There can't be two of you.

Edward almost smiles at his characterization...but...

                       EDWARD
        This is serious business. We're here
        to win a war.

                       RAY BROCCO
        Just the two of us?

The PHONE rings. They both look at it.

                       EDWARD
        Are you going to answer it?

67   CONTINUED: (2)   67

                    RAY BROCCO
          It depends if I'm working for you, or
          if I'm not...

Edward looks at him, studying him. After a moment:

                    EDWARD
          One of your jobs, Sergeant Brocco, is
          answering the telephone...And I prefer
          that you didn't wear your uniform.
          That we're as anonymous as possible.

                    RAY BROCCO
          Yes, sir.

And he answers the phone..."American Trade Bureau. Dry goods."

A68   INT. 1941, THE LONDON O.S.S. OFFICES - ANOTHER DAY   A68

Ray Brocco sits at his desk in a busy hall outside Edward's
office. Getting up he turns into the office...

B68   INT. 1941, EDWARD'S LONDON OFFICE THE O.S.S. - DAY   B68

Crowded with boxes and file cabinets, Edward, busy at work,
surrounded by papers, bent over his desk, writing something.

                    RAY BROCCO
          It's almost four...

                    EDWARD
          How do you spell "syphilis", one or
          two 'l's.'

                    RAY BROCCO
          Syphilis...One I think...I never had it.

Edward, hurrying, finishes, giving it to Ray.

                    EDWARD
          And I need word from our "son" in
          Berlin.

Ray nods and hurries out of the office. As Edward works...

68   INT. 1941, EDWARD'S O.S.S. OFFICE, LONDON - NIGHT   68

Edward, at desk, Ray by a "boarded" window to protect them
from a bomb shattering the glass...Listening to the RADIO, we
hear a BBC REPORTER:

                    BBC REPORTER
          "..Doctors in England today announced
          that medical records taken from Adolph
          Hitler's personal physician, Dr.
          Theodor Morrell, reveal that Mr.
          Hitler had contracted syphilis while
          serving in the German armed forces
          during World War I.
                    (MORE)

                                        (CONTINUED)

68   CONTINUED: 68

                           BBC REPORTER (CONT'D)
               Syphilis unless immediately treated
               causes a deterioration of the ability
               to reason, leads to severe
               disorientation, confusion, paranoia,
               and ultimately senility dementia and
               death..." "British medical experts say
               Mr. Hitler exhibits behavior related
               to the final stages of syphilis and
               his death could be imminent..."

Ray smiles...Edward is impassive. The phone RINGS. Ray answers.

                           RAY BROCCO
               Mr. Stickney is calling about a poetry
               class.

69   INT. 1941, THE LONDON PUB - NIGHT   69

The pub, mostly empty, a radio playing the BBC.   In the far
corner, are Edward and Dr. Fredericks.

                           DR. FREDERICKS
               Syphilis is inspired.   The Fuhrer's
               own staff will wonder if it's safe to
               have contact with him...

A Man in his early thirties, tailored, handsome, with a
charismatic, charming way about him, the English equivalent
of a "Yalie," but smarter, Arch Cummings, comes into the bar,
crossing to them. He has a perceptible stutter.

                           ARCH CUMMINGS
               Is it unusually smokey out, or is it
               just me? The coal dust...
                   (takes off coat)
               You can't help but get dust on
               everything.
                   (wiping dust off his coat, smiles)
               The Germans are wreaking havoc with my
               cleaning allowance.
                   (ingratiating, offering his hand)
               You must be young Edward. Dr.
               Fredericks has told me so much about
               you. Arch Cummings, Mr. Wilson.

Edward shakes his hand... pleased at meeting him...

                           ARCH CUMMINGS (CONT'D)
               How are you surviving the bombs? Try
               not to count the seconds before each
               blast. (smiles) It can reek havoc with
               your sleep. The most dangerous part
               is to be hit by shattering glass.
               What I do is put a pillow to cover my
               genitals. (he laughs) They are the
               only thing worth protecting. I would
               prefer to be dead without them anyway.

Edward appreciates his humor.

                           ARCH CUMMINGS (CONT'D)
               I understand we're of a like mind on
               many things... good schoolboys, Yale
               and Cambridge, and all that...

                                                    (CONTINUED)

And suddenly Arch closes his eyes, smiling... as he...

                    ARCH CUMMINGS (CONT'D)
          Give me any letter and I'll name at
          least 10 objects in this room that
          begins with it.

                    EDWARD
          The letter "P".

                    ARCH CUMMINGS
          Pewter mugs. A baby pram. Photographs
          of boxers.

Edward looks and sees Pewter mugs above the bar, a woman at a
table drinking, her baby in a pram, photographs of boxers.
One has the name John Henry Booth.

                    ARCH CUMMINGS (CONT'D)
          A fire poker. A pack of cigarettes.
          Picks for your teeth. Two pensioners.
          Porcelain penguins, pistol, plane,
          pony, platter of pears. How many is
          that?

We see all that... He opens his eyes and smiles. Edward is
impressed by his cleverness...except for...

                    EDWARD
          That's 10, but you missed the Painting
          of the river over the fireplace.

                    ARCH CUMMINGS
               (looks around to see...)
          I didn't...?

                    EDWARD
          There isn't one.

Arch Cummings laughs hard at being dunned.

                    EDWARD (CONT'D)
          Don't be fooled by what's not there.

                    ARCH CUMMINGS
          Or what seems to be there. Well done.
          Well done. Walter said how much I
          would like you. How much we're alike.
          Dreamers. They say to be an
          exceptional intelligence officer you
          must have a steady mind, an unwavering
          sense of belief in what you are doing,
          and to be... (smiling) A hopeless
          romantic.

Beethoven's Fifth Symphony plays, getting their attention...
After some preliminary headline news...

(CONTINUED)

69   CONTINUED: (2)   69

> BBC REPORTER (OVER)
> In other reportings...A Mother in
> Gloucester had asked us yesterday to
> read a letter to her beloved son in
> Berlin..."Dear Martin, it has been a
> long, cold winter but our hearts are
> warmed by thoughts of you..Each day we
> wait for the Postman to see what news
> he will deliver.." Martin answered his
> mother today, hoping she is quite well,
> and telling her, in case of rain, she
> might want to find a barrel-maker."

> EDWARD
> (thinking)
> A barrel maker's known as a Cooper
> here, isn't he?

> DR. FREDERICKS
> Lord Cooper. Bloody traitor.

70   EXT. 1941, FOREIGN OFFICE - ANOTHER NIGHT   70

A chauffeured Car waits by a large GOVERNMENT BUILDING. A MAN
in a BOWLER hat exits building and gets in his car. LORD
COOPER turns and sees Arch Cummings get into his car.

A71   INT. 1941, LORD COOPER'S CAR - NIGHT   A71

> LORD COOPER
> What do you think you're doing?

> ARCH CUMMINGS
> Good evening, Lord Cooper. I have
> something for you.

Arch shows him some credentials and SURVEILLANCE PHOTOS. LORD
COOPER LOADING A DEAD DROP, A GERMAN SPY CLEARING THE DEAD
DROP, A SHOT OF A CHALK MARK ON A MAILBOX, THEIR 'SIGNAL SITE.

> LORD COOPER
> (to his driver)
> Henry, if you don't mind waiting a
> moment.

> ARCH CUMMINGS
> We know you've been passing
> information to the German High
> Command...

B71   INT. 1941 DR. FREDERICKS CAR, LONDON - NIGHT   B71

Edward and Dr. Fredericks can see the backs of their heads...

> DR. FREDERICKS
> Remember, it is never a two way
> discussion...Never give anybody time
> to think...

C71   INT. 1941, LORD COOPER'S CAR, LONDON - NIGHT   C71

                    ARCH CUMMINGS
          Now, I'm going to offer you one of
          two choices... Either you will be
          executed for treason or you will
          continue to spy for the enemy and
          provide them with the information we
          provide you with... And by the end of
          the war you can tell your children
          you were a genuine war hero.

Sounds of APPROACHING AIRPLANES. They look up. SIRENS SOUND.
City's lights go out.

                    LORD COOPER
          (panicked)
          For godsake. We need to find cover.
          There's a shelter--

                    ARCH CUMMINGS
          I'm afraid, my dear lord, God isn't
          listening....

He starts out of the car, but Arch grabs him. BUZZ BOMBS
whistle as they fall, then their horrible silence before
exploding... Cummings gives him a piece of paper.

                    DR. FREDERICKS
          (to Edward by way of
            instruction)
          Always give your credentials... and
          set the tone for the discussion... And
          quickly come to the point...

                    ARCH CUMMINGS
          You are going to pass this on to your
          German friends... And if I find out it
          wasn't done, there won't be a second
          chance, and you'll quite simply be
          hanged as a spy. Do you understand,
          your Lordship? Once more and out.

They look at each other. Arch Cummings lets go, opens the
door, and Lord Cooper hurries off to shelter.

D71   INT. 1941, DR. FREDERICKS' CAR LONDON - NIGHT   D71

Edward and Fredericks watch Lord Cooper disappear into the dark.

                    EDWARD
          How do we know he won't be working for
          two masters?

                    DR. FREDERICKS
          Precisely. We don't.

71   INT. 1941, EDWARD'S O.S.S. OFFICE, LONDON - LATE NIGHT   71

Edward looks out at London. Ray, in overcoat, comes to the door.

                                          (CONTINUED)

71   CONTINUED:

                         RAY BROCCO
              Do you need me for anything else
              tonight?

Edward, without turning, shakes "no." The phone RINGS.

                         RAY BROCCO (CONT'D)
              American Trade Bureau. No, Mr. Carlson
              just left for the night... May I ask
              who's calling?... It's for you,
              overseas Mother, a Senator Russell.

                         EDWARD
              Hello... Yes, I can hear you... Thank
              you for telling me. Give her my love.
              I will try to arrange a call.

A moment. He hangs up. He bends to read some papers...

                         RAY BROCCO
              Is anything wrong?

                         EDWARD
                    (shy, smiles)
              We had a boy.

                         RAY BROCCO
              I didn't even know you were
              married... Well, that's great news...
              Let's have a drink, celebrate...

Ray takes a bottle from a drawer, pouring drinks in paper cups.

                         RAY BROCCO (CONT'D)
              I remember my little boy's first pair
              of shoes. The tiny brown laces...Pink
              toes...To a long and healthy life.

                         EDWARD
              A long and healthy life.

They touch cups. They drink. It's quiet.

                         RAY BROCCO
              Hopefully, one day we'll be drinking
              to our grandchildren. What's his name?

                         EDWARD
              I don't know.

72   INT. 1941, THE CAMBRIDGE CLUB, LONDON - DAY   72

An elegant dining room in an old English Men's Club. Edward
is shown to a table. Arch Cummings waits for him.

                         ARCH CUMMINGS
              I heard the good news. A son. How
              lovely. (giving him a gift) When he's
              old enough you can read it to him.

Edward looks at it, a very old book.

                                                           (CONTINUED)

                         ARCH CUMMINGS (CONT'D)
                    It's a first edition. Charles
                    Dickens. "A Christmas Carol." It was
                    my father's. He would read it to me
                    when I was a boy.

                         EDWARD
                         (genuinely touched)
                    I couldn't.

                         ARCH CUMMINGS
                    We are friends. Hopeless romantics. I
                    insist...

Edward is appropriately grateful. They sit down. Edward
appreciates his humor. A waiter brings them some tea.

                         ARCH CUMMINGS (CONT'D)
                    I had an unfortunate discovery
                    today... A man that works for me, sat
                    just outside my door... I found out
                    that he had given a rose to a woman
                    with a small note... the rose was
                    quite lovely... an Abyssinian rose.
                    It's stem neatly wrapped in paper
                    silk. All quite beautiful and
                    touching, save for the fact that the
                    paper was filled with secret writing
                    for her German friends, detailing
                    changes to the American order of
                    battle here...He was her mole. You
                    just can't trust anyone no matter how
                    well you think you know them... Your
                    best friend while he is smiling and
                    giving you a gift, a pat on the back,
                    when you are not looking, could be
                    taking your very soul... How did the
                    Irish poet say it, "Aye a friend for
                    today is tomorrow's heartbreak." Do
                    you have many friends?

                         EDWARD
                    No. Not many.

                         ARCH CUMMINGS
                    In our profession it's best that way.
                    Do you know what my deepest fear
                    is...? I will end up a man without a
                    country, friendless, completely alone.

They're quiet, drinking their tea. Arch laughs, enjoying him.
A Butler brings Arch a message. He reads, nods. After a
moment:

                         ARCH CUMMINGS (CONT'D)
                    I think you two know each other...

Edward sees RICHARD HAYES coming to their table...

                         EDWARD
                    Richard.

(CONTINUED)

                    RICHARD HAYES
          Edward.

                    ARCH CUMMINGS
          Mr. Hayes has come over to work with
          us in Special Operations. I hope you
          don't mind, I invited him to join our
          conversation...

He offers his hand. Edward shakes it, still no love lost.
Hayes sits down. Arch looks around, then sits closer...

                    ARCH CUMMINGS (CONT'D)
          I'm afraid our dear "English teacher"
          has a bad habit of making "easy"
          friendships. You know, of course,
          about his particular sexual tastes.

                    EDWARD
          Why would I know about that?

                    RICHARD HAYES
          You were good friends, an
          impressionable poetry student once.

                    EDWARD
          Not that impressionable.

                    ARCH CUMMINGS
          I am as obliged to him as the next man.
          He is my mentor. My father confessor.
          My teacher... (troubled) I am afraid he
          has not been very discriminating in his
          partners. Some people are extremely
          worried about his "exposure..."

He's quiet, this is not easy for him...

                    ARCH CUMMINGS (CONT'D)
          Now if you'll excuse me gentlemen,
          I'll let you renew your
          acquaintance... (frowns, concerned)
          I hope you two can help sort this
          rather delicate matter out for us.

And getting up he goes to another table, talking to a man...

                    EDWARD
          It seems to me to be a problem for the
          British... Why are we involved?

                    RICHARD HAYES
          The British are a civilized people.
          (wry) They don't eat their own...
          They have somebody do it for them.

                    EDWARD
          Why are you telling me this?

                    RICHARD HAYES
          I'm giving you the opportunity to handle
          it, Edward... Or somebody else will.

They look at each other... Edward has been put on notice...

>   EDWARD
>   If you'll excuse me... I have things
>   to do...

>   ARCH CUMMINGS
>   (stopping him, quietly)
>   I'm sorry you have been brought into
>   this. (genuinely seeming sorry) If the
>   headmaster won't listen to reason you
>   might want to tie your shoe... (and a
>   beat) I'm sorry it has to be this way.
>   Truly sorry. It's not something I'm
>   happy about having to be doing.
>   (softly) Ours is not a business for
>   the faint of heart.

Edward nods, looks at him, and leaves. He slows on his way
out, looking back at them, reading Richards' lips.

>   RICHARD HAYES
>   "...I don't think he has the heart for
>   this work..."

73   INT. 1941, EDWARD'S O.S.S OFFICE, LONDON - NIGHT, LATER   73

Edward, on cot, staring out window. The rumble of bombs, lights
fade in the distance. Phone RINGS. Edward gets it. OPERATOR'S
VOICE: "Your party is on the line... Your call will be ended in
exactly five minutes... I'll need to stay on the line." Then:

>   EDWARD
>   Hello... Clover...? It's Edward.
>   (beat, smiles)
>   Was that the baby crying?

A74   INT. 1941, SOLARIUM, THE RUSSELL ESTATE, CT - DAY   A74

Clover in bed, holding their new baby...the baby crying.

>   CLOVER
>   Yes, he has a healthy set of lungs.

B74   INT. 1941, EDWARD'S O.S.S. OFFICE, LONDON - NIGHT   B74

Edward in his office. We will go back and forth between them,
Edward in his dark office, Clover in her hospital bed...

>   EDWARD
>   How are you?

>   CLOVER
>   ...I feel fine... just tired... He
>   didn't seem to want to be born.

>   EDWARD
>   What? Say again? The baby -- ? Is he ?

And there's the awkwardness of a new father. Pure emotion...

>   CLOVER
>   He's completely healthy... He has
>   everything where it's supposed to be.

>   EDWARD
>   Say again...? What names have you
>   thought about?

>   CLOVER
>   I can't decide.

>   EDWARD
>   Would you mind if we called him
>   Edward? Edward Jr?

>   CLOVER
>   Edward. Yes. I like that. "Edward."
>   It's very regal. A king's name.

>   EDWARD
>   That's what I was thinking. Fit for a
>   king.

They're quiet. After some moments:

>   CLOVER
>   How is your work going? Are you saving
>   the world? Keeping us safe?

>   EDWARD
>   (awkwardly, serious)
>   Sometimes...(changing subject) Does he
>   have a lot of hair? What color are his
>   eyes?

As he continues on the phone in the dark office...the operator
comes on the line, "Sorry sir, your five minutes are up."

>   EDWARD (CONT'D)
>   I love you.

74   EXT. 1941, AN OLD COURTYARD, LONDON - NIGHT   74

We see Edward and Dr. Fredericks walking home.

>   EDWARD
>   ...Have you thought about going back
>   to teaching full time...?

>   DR. FREDERICKS
>   Arch Cummings is an ambitious young
>   man. He's never liked having a
>   Headmaster. He wants to be the
>   Headmaster himself. Be very careful,
>   Edward, "ambition" is an overly praised
>   attribute.

Edward is quiet. They stop. After a beat:

>   DR. FREDERICKS (CONT'D)
>   He's saying they're concerned about my
>   personal "associations?" Aren't they?
>   (MORE)

(CONTINUED)

                         DR. FREDERICKS (CONT'D)
                    Boys to "men." The Cambridge lads stick
                    together like glue. I'm far more
                    democratic in my tastes than they
                    prefer. They prefer pressed trousers
                    and proper buttons... I've done all the
                    teaching I intend to. I'm afraid this
                    is who I am, Edward. I'll suffer that.

They look at each other.

                         EDWARD
                    Please -- You've given all the service
                    you can. It's time to retire.

Dr. Fredericks is silent. Edward nods, nothing left to do.

                         DR. FREDERICKS
                    Did you know Edward, your shoe seems
                    to be untied.

                         EDWARD
                    I must have been in a hurry...

                         DR. FREDERICKS
                    The good schoolboy will be close by.
                    He'll want to know my response. I would
                    understand if you want to tie your shoe,
                    Edward. It's a dirty business. Gentleman
                    have short memories. I have been a part
                    of it for far too long.

Edward is quiet, well aware of his untied shoelace. But he
can't do it. Dr. Fredericks nods, appreciating his loyalty.
He bends to tie Edward's worn shoes. As if passing the mantle:

                         DR. FREDERICKS (CONT'D)
                    You might want to think about getting some
                    new shoes, Edward... There's a wonderful
                    shop in St. James. A Mr. Pettibone's. He's
                    a bootmaker to the King.

And finished tying Edward's shoe, he straightens.

                         DR. FREDERICKS (CONT'D)
                    We are all, in our own way, Edward,
                    just bootmakers to kings...

He looks at Edward. He puts his cane fondly on his shoulder.

                         DR. FREDERICKS (CONT'D)
                    Get out while you still can. While
                    you still have a soul. While you
                    still believe...

Dr. Fredericks turns and walks off, his cane tapping the
ground. Edward watches him go, seeing him come to the end of
street, where MEN are standing in doorways...a pickup area. A
YOUNG MAN motions to him. Dr. Fredericks stops to talk with
him in doorway. They laugh. The Young Man whispers something.
Dr. Fredericks nods. They walk off, talking intimately, the
man's arm on Fredericks' waist, taking him around side of
building. Realizing the set-up, Edward starts after them. He
runs down block, around the building, towards the Thames...

                                                        (CONTINUED)

74   CONTINUED: (2)   74

The shadows of a narrow alley, empty, except for Fredrick's
cane. He hears sounds of Fredrick's blood chilling screams. A
moment and the Young Man, along with other Men, push Dr.
Fredericks' body into the water. As they go, he throws the
cane in the river. Hearing footsteps echo, Edward turns and
sees Arch Cummings.

                    ARCH CUMMINGS
          I am terribly sorry, Edward...
          He knew too much...

And turning, he walks off. As Edward stands in the shadows
under the bridge... Edward, not so young anymore...

A75   INT. 1941, EDWARD'S O.S.S. OFFICE, LONDON - NIGHT   A75

Edward on a cot in dark office, trying to sleep. A RADIO plays
music, which becomes news. Among the stories, "An unidentified
man's body washed ashore on the East End of the Thames this
evening." "Police are asking for any missing persons." Music
plays again...Edward listens to the music, no so young anymore.

75   EXT. 1961, EDWARD'S SUBURBAN STREET, VIRGINIA - NIGHT 75

"Friday, April 21, 1961." A Bus stops. Edward, in raincoat,
with briefcase, gets off. He walks along suburban street, porch
lights on, children riding bikes, their voices carrying. He
goes up the walk to his front door. Sensing someone, he turns
to see Hayes in the dark, on porch.

                    RICHARD HAYES
          Hello, Edward.

                    EDWARD
          What are you doing here?

Hayes doesn't say anything.

                    RICHARD HAYES
          There were only a handful of us...
          until moment zero, who knew where we
          were going to land in Cuba... One of
          us couldn't keep a secret...
          I know it wasn't me.

                    EDWARD
          I want you to leave Mr. Hayes. This
          is my home.

                    RICHARD HAYES
          Our friend upstairs, Mr. Allen, asked
          me for a list of personnel who
          participated in the operation. I don't
          have one. I said you would.

Edward is quiet.

                    RICHARD HAYES (CONT'D)
          He's trying to make a case for
          himself...that mistakes were made he
          had nothing to do with...You know,
          Mother, "The first to forget is the
          last to know..."

                                              (CONTINUED)

                           EDWARD
             Tell Mr. Allen I'll bring him the list
             personally.

                           RICHARD HAYES
             I "captured" a copy of a draft letter
             of his...His proposed housecleaning.
             One of his proposals is reassigning you
             to a "vacant" desk. Another is to
             reassign me to Records Integration. Can
             you imagine, fucking "R.I."?

Edward doesn't say anything.

                           RICHARD HAYES (CONT'D)
             We're in the same boat together,
             Mother. A leaking boat...

                           EDWARD
             Don't ever think we're in the same
             boat, Mr. Hayes.

                           RICHARD HAYES
             We're either going to sink or swim,
             together, Mother...I'll watch your
             back, you watch mine..."People like
             us," we don't let each other drown.

Edward is quiet. Richard looks around. Without any sympathy...

                           RICHARD HAYES (CONT'D)
             Edward is gone. Your wife lives in
             Phoenix. You must be lonely without
             your family...Why have a family at
             all?

And Richard goes, driving away. Edward looks at the street,
porch lights on, kids' voices on bikes, the "normal" lives...

A76   INT. 1961, EDWARD'S HOUSE, BEDROOM - NIGHT - APRIL 21   A76

Edward, 40, buttons his pajamas, getting ready for bed. A TV
is on to JFK denying U.S. involvement with the Bay of Pigs.
And as Edward listens to the President lie to America...

76   OMITTED   76

77   EXT. 1945, BERLIN STREET - DAY   77

                           PHILIP ALLEN (OVER)
             Welcome to Berlin.

Edward follows Philip Allen down a war-torn Berlin street.

                           PHILIP ALLEN (CONT'D)
             How are Clover and your little boy?

                           EDWARD
             They're well, thank you. He's nearly
             five.

                                                    (CONTINUED)

> PHILIP ALLEN
> You made quite a name for yourself in
> London. The General is still smiling.

> EDWARD
> Thank you. I did the best I could.

> PHILIP ALLEN
> (whispers)
> Can you keep a secret?

He takes out a box of chocolates.

> PHILIP ALLEN (CONT'D)
> They are from Switzerland. I had them
> sent with the pouch.

He offers one to Edward. Edward shakes "no." Philip takes one.

> PHILIP ALLEN (CONT'D)
> They are a weakness of mine. When I
> was a child my mother would always
> reward me with a chocolate. (winks)
> It's a dreadful habit.

> EDWARD
> (a rare smile)
> Chocolates? Or seeking approval?

> PHIILIP ALLEN
> (laughs)
> Both.

They turn to see a group of American soldiers walk by a group
of Russian soldiers, a slight tension between them...Philip
lights his pipe and watches.

> PHILIP ALLEN
> The world war is over... The war for
> the world has just begun...In every
> liberated country there will be a
> battle between us and the Russians for
> the hearts and minds.
> (whispering)
> Since we dropped the bomb, the
> Russians are feeling a little short
> between the legs....They are still in
> the nineteenth century... Beets and
> potatoes... That will change
> dramatically... Right now they're
> grabbing up territory, taking home
> with them every scientist they can
> steal... In a few years they'll have
> the bomb... Communism is a spreading
> cancer... We have to isolate them
> wherever they are... We have to get
> anyone that can be useful to us out of
> Berlin before they do...

They turn and watch a few Russian Guards finish raising a
Russian Flag over a building...

                         PHILIP ALLEN (CONT'D)
              Churchill was right, we shouldn't have
              stopped stop marching until we reached
              Moscow. (Offers) You sure you don't
              want a chocolate?

Edward shakes "No, thank you," as Phillip takes another
one...A few German kids beg for chocolate.

                         PHILIP ALLEN (CONT'D)
              One chocolate, for all three to share.

78   INT. 1945, EDWARD'S O.S.S. OFFICE, BERLIN, GERMANY - DAY   78

A former Nazi building. Edward, incongruous, sits hunched
over paperwork in large dark office, still replete with
ornate trappings from the Nazi regime, the molding on his
desk twin eagles... Ray Brocco shows in a Man in a tired
suit, and a young, pretty, dark haired woman, HANNA SCHILLER.

                         RAY BROCCO
              Mr. Carlson, this is Herr Franck...
              Fraulein Schiller has been cleared to
              work as our interpreter...

Edward looks up at them. He sees she's wearing a hearing-aid,
the bulky kind with the oversized ear-piece.

                         EDWARD
              Welcome Fraulein Schiff. I speak some
              German, but very little.

Edward motions them to sit. The Man says something in German.

                         HANNA
              ...He was an officer in the Abwehr,
              German Military Intelligence... He
              says he knows the locations of certain
              Nazi V2 rocket scientists in hiding...
              Particularly a Rudolph von Schoen...

                         EDWARD
              Where do you want to go?

The Man says something in quick German.

                         HANNA
              He said Chicago. He has relatives there.

                         EDWARD
              Tell him if he gives us the names and
              locations of the scientists I will
              arrange an exit visa for him...

Hanna repeats it in German. The Man nods he will, gets up,
stiffly nods to Edward, and leaves. Edward whispers to Ray...

                         EDWARD (CONT'D)
              Once he's served his purpose hand him
              over to the Nazi catchers...

Ray nods and leaves. Hanna gets up.

                                                      (CONTINUED)

78   CONTINUED: 78

                              HANNA
                    An ex-Waffen S.S. Group Commander
                    would like to speak with you about
                    asylum.

          Edward nods. She starts to go. He looks at her hearing-aid.
          Seeing his look she pushes some hair over it, covering it...

                              HANNA (CONT'D)
                    It is very ugly, isn't it?

                              EDWARD
                    It's not supposed to be jewelry.

          She smiles, appreciative... An awkward quiet... Then:

                              HANNA
                    This... My father played piano in the
                    Berlin Symphony. The orchestra was
                    "asked" to join the Nazi party. He
                    refused. The SS visited us. They made
                    my father sit in a chair. They turned
                    on the victrola, a piece by Schumann my
                    father had played with the symphony.
                    While the recording played, they raped
                    me. When they were finished one of them
                    put a gun up to my head, and fired once
                    by each ear... So that I could never
                    hear my father's music ever again... I
                    lost the sound in one ear altogether...
                    I can hear with the help of the
                    apparatus out of this ear... But they
                    say in a year or so...

                              EDWARD
                    You forget it is even there.

          Ray Brocco comes back into the office, and whispers to Edward:

                              RAY BROCCO
                    The Russians are interested in making
                    a prisoner swap.

79   INT. 1945, A CATHEDRAL IN BERLIN - DAY   79

          A large old Cathedral, holes in the walls from Allied bombs.
          Ray comes inside and crosses into a CONFESSIONAL.

80   INT. 1945, THE CONFESSIONAL, A CATHEDRAL IN BERLIN - DAY 80

          Some moments, and the Priest's door opens. A Man's figure,
          behind the mesh, sits down...

                              THE TARTAR
                    Mr. Wilson...?

                              RAY BROCCO
                    Mr. Siyanko...?

                                                          (CONTINUED)

80   CONTINUED: 80

                              THE TARTAR
                    We are prepared to offer you some
                    Jewish scientists that were liberated
                    in the East for some Nazi scientists
                    you have here in Berlin...

He passes a list of names under the mesh screen to Ray...

                              RAY BROCCO
                    These are the names we are willing to
                    discuss...

In return, Ray passes a list of names to the man...

81   INT. 1945, THE CATHEDRAL IN BERLIN - DAY   81

There's a soft echo as a few penitents pray. Edward sits in a
pew toward the back, quietly watching the Confessional.

                         A MAN'S VOICE (OVER)
                    Hello, Mother...

Edward sees sitting in a pew across from him, a slender,
handsome Man in a tailored suit in his early thirties, with
the fine features of a ballet dancer and the cold, forgotten
soul of a chess player... Stas Siyanko.

                              STAS SIYANKO
                    I understand your cryptonym for me is
                    "Ulysses." Is that for the James Joyce
                    book or the Greek myth?

                              EDWARD
                    What would you prefer?

Stas smiles.

                              STAS SIYANKO
                    Do you know what our cryptonym is for
                    you...? Mother.

Stas gets up to sit beside Edward.

                         STAS SIYANKO (CONT'D)
                    I could only locate one photograph of
                    you... You were just a Freshman at
                    Prep school... the poetry society.

                              EDWARD
                    The only photograph we have of you is
                    from the Young Pioneers... when you
                    were thirteen... the chess club...

                              STAS SIYANKO
                    I guess we are both camera shy... It
                    is curious knowing someone without a
                    face... to know every detail, every
                    nuance of a man's life, before you
                    have even looked him in the eye...

They look each other in the eye. After some moments:

                                                          (CONTINUED)

81   CONTINUED:

>   STAS SIYANKO (CONT'D)
> ...I took the first hot bath yesterday
> I've taken in three years -- since the
> siege of Stalingrad... I sat for
> hours, looking out the window,
> soaking... There is nothing like the
> light in Berlin... clear and
> haunting...

Edward looks at Stas, rubbing his hands for warmth...

>   STAS SIYANKO (CONT'D)
> When I was a soldier, My fingers were
> frost bitten. When I get cold, there
> is a shooting pain.

>   EDWARD
>   (smiling)
> Maybe you shouldn't live in Russia.

>   STAS SIYANKO
> We all have our weaknesses. What is
> yours, Mother?

Edward doesn't say anything.

>   STAS SIYANKO (CONT'D)
> It is interesting to me how both of
> our countries must now take a global
> view.... a battleground for ideas...
> When you talk to Arch Cummings again
> will you give him my best... we spent
> a wonderful summer at Cambridge
> together...Is he still so fascinated
> with moles? A spy under every bed...?

After some moments...

>   STAS SIYANKO (CONT'D)
>   (smiles)
> I had heard you were silent. "Made of
> stone," they said. What is the
> expression, "The silence is
> deafening?" You are going to be a
> formidable adversary, Mother.

>   EDWARD
> I didn't know we were adversaries yet,
> Ulysses. I thought we were allies.

>   STAS SIYANKO
> Oh, I wanted to show you, something...

He takes a small PHOTOGRAPH out of his wallet, and shows it
to him. A photograph of a small CHILD on a field trip at the
zoo, looking at a caged animal.

>   STAS SIYANKO (CONT'D)
> He's quite lovely, isn't he...?

Edward doesn't say anything...

(CONTINUED)

81   CONTINUED: (2)   81

                              STAS SIYANKO (CONT'D)
                     You are welcome to keep it...After
                     all, it is your son.

Edward still doesn't say anything. The Confessional door
opens, and Stas's alter ego, his TARTAR, comes out. He
leaves the church, and Stas gets up to go.

                              STAS SIYANKO (CONT'D)
                     Be well, Mother... I look forward to
                     our association. I hope it lasts for a
                     long time.

They look each other in the eye... and Stas leaves.

82   INT. 1945, EDWARD'S O.S.S OFFICE, BERLIN - NIGHT, LATE   82

Edward, bent over desk, looking at son's photo. He takes up
the phone, asks for a number, and hangs up...The phone rings:

                              EDWARD
                     Hello...

And we hear a little boy's voice:

                              EDWARD JR. (V.O.)
                     Who is this?

                              EDWARD
                     Who is this?

                              EDWARD JR. (V.O.)
                     This is Edward!

Edward smiles.

                              EDWARD
                     How old are you?

                              EDWARD JR. (V.O.)
                     Four and three-quarters.

                              EDWARD
                     You're four and three-quarters? You're
                     a big boy.

                              EDWARD JR. (V.O.)
                     I'm bigger than Andrew and he's six.

Edward laughs...

                              EDWARD
                     Is your mother there...?

His words are garbled by the static...

                              EDWARD JR.
                     What did you say?

                              EDWARD
                     Is your mother home?

                                                          (CONTINUED)

                  EDWARD JR. (V.O.)
        She's getting dressed to go out with
        her friend.

Before Edward can say anything else, the little boy says...

                  EDWARD JR. (V.O.) (CONT'D)
        He has a new car... He let me drive
        with him... He plays a horn...

And the phone has been taken away from him...

                  A WOMAN'S VOICE
        This is Edna, I'm Mrs. Wilson's Nanny.
        Who is calling, please?

                  EDWARD
          (quietly)
        I'll call again.

He presses a button to disconnect. The phone rings right away.

                  AN OPERATOR'S VOICE
        Are you finished with your call, sir?

                  EDWARD
        Yes. Yes, I'm finished.

He quietly hangs up. Edward alone with his boy's photo. A
sound, and he sees Hanna, in a raincoat, has stopped in the
doorway. He turns the photo over.

                  HANNA
        Pardon me... Do you need me for
        anything else?

He shakes "no."

                  HANNA (CONT'D)
        Gute nacht...

                  EDWARD
        Gute Nacht.

He nods. She turns to leave. Edward alone at his desk.

                  HANNA (OVER)
        Do you ever eat, Mr. Carlson?

He sees she's come back...

                  HANNA (CONT'D)
        I like to cook... Would you like, how
        do you call it, a "cooked-at-home
        meal?"

She self-consciously pushes her hair over her hearing-aid...

83   INT. 1945, HANNA'S APARTMENT, BERLIN - NIGHT   83

Edward and Hanna have finished dinner. Hanna does the dishes in
a small kitchen, Edward sits at table with a bottle of wine.

                    HANNA
          Have you ever read Ovid,
          "Metamorphosis," in the original
          Latin...? It's quite beautiful...

She quotes from Ovid's Metamorphosis..."

                    HANNA (CONT'D)
          "Ego pulveris hausti ostendens cumulum,
          quot haberet corpora pulvis,
          tot mihi natales contingere vana rogavi;

Edward, a step ahead, picks up where she left off...

                    EDWARD
          "Excidit, ut peterem iuvenes quoque
          protinus annos." (and then
          translating:) "I grabbed a pile of
          dust, and holding it up, foolishly
          asked for as many birthdays as the
          grains of dust...I forgot to ask that
          they might be years of youth."

                    HANNA
              (laughs)
          Bravo. You are always one step ahead
          of me...

He smiles, the last hint of a boy. She turns to the table to
take up some of the dishes... He looks at her...

                    HANNA (CONT'D)
          You have a way of looking at someone..
          It gets, how do you say it, "in your
          skin..."

                    EDWARD
          Under your skin...I should be going...

He gets up. There's an uncomfortable moment. She self-
consciously pushes her hair over her hearing-aid...

                    HANNA
              (in german)
          Would you like to stay?

                    EDWARD
              (hesitates, in German)
          Would you like me to?

                    HANNA
              (in german)
          I would like you to very much...

84   INT. 1945, HANNA'S APARTMENT - NIGHT, LATER   84

Edward and Hanna lay close together in bed. Edward is
uncharacteristically intimate, particularly vulnerable...

                    EDWARD
          ...I hardly knew her... I've never met
          my little boy...

A moment. She looks at him, into his boy's eyes, and says...

                    HANNA
          You are safe here with me...

She reaches to hold him... He hesitates, then gives in to her.

85   INT. 1945, HANNA'S APARTMENT - MORNING   85

Edward lays in bed, peaceful, the shower running... Edward can
see Hanna in the shower, and her HEARING-AID on the sink top.
She gets out of the shower, drying... turning to Edward...

                    HANNA
          Would you like to go somewhere
          together? The lakes in Bavaria are
          still beautiful. There was an inn
          there before the war where the sheets
          smelled like fresh flowers and they
          served breakfast in bed all day.

He smiles at the idea. She turns, drying, happily humming to
herself. Edward quietly watches her. He looks at hearing-aid,
then at Hanna, her back to him... At the hearing-aid once
more. He doesn't really want to know, but he has to:

                    EDWARD
          Hanna...

Hanna turns... then turns back to drying herself. Covering...
But it's all too late. As she pretends nothing's changed, his
distant eyes can't hide his heartache... the betrayal...

86   INT. 1945, A HOTEL IN BERLIN - DUSK   86

Stas in bathtub, looking at the light of Berlin... A knock: A
Room Service Man comes in. He puts the tray by the tub and
leaves. Stas pours the tea... There's something inside. He
opens the teapot and sees Hanna's HEARING-AID...

87   INT. 1945, HANNA'S APARTMENT, BERLIN - DUSK   87

Hanna, by her closet, getting dressed. The bedroom door
opens... She turns, seeing Stas's Tartar come into bedroom.
Before she can say speak, she's shot in the head, falling to
the floor. The Tartar leaves as Hanna lays there, her blood
soaking the carpet...the Cold War begun.

A88   EXT. BALCONY OF EDWARD'S OFFICE, BERLIN - DUSK   A88

The last gasp of light. Edward in his overcoat, wind blowing his hair, silently standing on the balcony off his office, looking out at Berlin. And Ray comes outside. He whispers something in Edward's ear. Edward nods.

>   EDWARD
>   (chilling)
>   I let a stranger in our house...

And he's closed what's left of his heart. Ray is quiet. He turns back inside and as Edward stands on the balcony...

88   EXT. 1946, EDWARD'S SUBURBAN STREET, ALEXANDRIA, VA - DAY 88

A taxi comes along a suburban street, a housing tract apart of the postwar American boom. The taxi, looking for an address, comes to the just built two-story colonial, slowing, then driving past. It stops, as if somebody were making up their mind, then backs up, stopping at the house. Edward gets out as the Driver brings his suitcase and leaves. Gathering his courage, Edward starts up the walk. A little Boy, Edward JR., comes running from around side of house. Seeing him, he slows.

>   EDWARD
>   Hello. Are you Edward?

Edward Jr., shy, runs back into the house.

89   INT. 1946, EDWARD'S SUBURBAN HOUSE, VIRGINIA - DAY   89

Edward Jr. runs into the house as Edward puts down his suitcase in the foyer.

>   EDWARD JR.
>   Mother, father's here...

Clover comes into the foyer...

>   CLOVER
>   Hello Edward.

>   EDWARD
>   Hello, Clover.

The girl that was once "Clover" is gone... a single, practical woman in her place.

>   CLOVER
>   I like to be called Margaret now...

He nods, respecting her wishes. They look at each other... after all the years...

>   CLOVER (CONT'D)
>   It's nice to see you again, Edward.

>   EDWARD
>   It's nice to see you again, too...
>   (looking around him, awkward)
>   It's a lovely house.

(CONTINUED)

89   CONTINUED:

                          CLOVER
               I've tried to make it a home.

There's an awkward quiet. Edward Jr. comes in and goes to
shyly stand with his mother, holding onto her dress.

                          EDWARD
               I made this especially for you.

He gives him a small SHIP IN A BOTTLE. The little Boy fingers
the bottle, looking inside as Edward describes it to him.
Edward looks at Clover, his son... Despite how new everything
is:

                          EDWARD (CONT'D)
               It's good to be home.

90   INT. 1946, EDWARD'S SUBURBAN HOUSE, BEDROOM - NIGHT   90

Clover lies in bed. Edward, carrying suitcase, comes into
room. There's an awkwardness, two strangers.

                          CLOVER
               If you don't mind -- I'd like us to
               sleep in separate beds for a
               while...until we know each other again
               I've made up the spare room...

                          EDWARD
               Alright.

He nods, he understands. He sits in a chair.

                          EDWARD (CONT'D)
               What do you hear from your brother
               John?

                          CLOVER
               John? I thought you knew. John was
               killed in Burma in 1944... Or should I
               say missing... his body was never
               recovered...

                          EDWARD
               You never mentioned it in any of your
               letters.

                          CLOVER
               There was nothing to say.

Edward is quiet, truly sorry. After some moments...

                          CLOVER (CONT'D)
               Six years is a long time. I've been
               very lonely... I was with a man once.

Edward looks at her. He understands.

                          CLOVER (CONT'D)
               He wasn't very interesting...
               Were you with anyone else?

                                              (CONTINUED)

He looks at her. He hesitates. And he shakes "yes."

                         EDWARD
              It was a mistake.

She looks at him, willing to:

                         CLOVER
              We don't have to be strangers. We can
              meet each other all over again,
              Edward.

                         EDWARD
              I would like that very much.

                         CLOVER
              Me too.

And they say goodnight...

91   INT. 1946, EDWARD'S SUBURBAN HOUSE, A SPARE ROOM - NIGHT   91

Edward unpacks, putting his things away. He takes out shoes of
fine English leather and looks at them. A slight sound. He
turns and sees Edward Jr. in the bedroom doorway watching him.

                         EDWARD
              Hello.

                         EDWARD JR.
              Hello.

                         EDWARD JR. (CONT'D)
              Mother said you were in the war. Did
              you fight? Did you kill anybody?

                         EDWARD
              I didn't kill anybody.

                         EDWARD JR.
              Good night.

                         EDWARD
              Good night.

Edward turns and puts his English shoes away in the closet.
As he closes the closet door, home from the war...

92   INT. 1947, EDWARD'S OFFICE, THE WAR DEPARTMENT - DAY   92

Painted on the glass of a door: "Strategic Services Unit."
Edward stands by a window looking outside. Like the country,
in postwar transition, a man without a mission...

93   EXT. 1947, EDWARD'S SUBURBAN STREET, ALEXANDRIA, VA - DUSK 93

Edward in raincoat, with briefcase, gets off Bus. Edward Jr.,
seven now, waits to greet him.

                         EDWARD JR.
              Father... Would you play catch with me?

                                                        (CONTINUED)

CONTINUED:

Clover, a cigarette and drink in hand, talks to other Young
Parents and Children in front of house. As Edward approaches:

                    CLOVER
          Someone's here to see you...

                    EDWARD JR.
          Can we play catch?

                    EDWARD
          Margaret...

                    CLOVER
          Sweetheart, your father has work to
          do. You stay with me.

                    EDWARD JR.
          Ok.

And Edward goes inside...

94   INT. 1947, EDWARD'S SUBURBAN HOUSE, ALEXANDRIA - EVENING   94

He puts his coat and briefcase down in the foyer. He turns
into the living room to see General WILLIAM SULLIVAN and a
redhaired MAN. The years have not treated the General well...

                    BILL SULLIVAN
          I'm sorry to barge in on you like
          this. Your wife kindly helped me to a
          drink.

Edward nods, sees a pair of crutches beside the General's chair.

                    BILL SULLIVAN (CONT'D)
          My fucking feet... They keep cutting
          off pieces of them... It's not
          dignified for a man to have to die
          from the feet up...

With some unseen signal, the redhaired Man gets up and goes to
a patio chair and sits. Edward sits across from the General.

                    BILL SULLIVAN (CONT'D)
          While everybody's been feeling good
          about themselves, the Soviets, without
          firing a shot, have taken over half
          the world... They're breathing down
          our necks... they'll be in our
          backyard before you know it.

Edward Jr. comes into the house, going into the den off living
room, playing with army men, talking to himself. Edward starts
to get up to have him leave, but Sullivan motions him not to
bother. He moves his chair closer to Edward.

                    BILL SULLIVAN (CONT'D)
          ...The president and his advisors
          don't seem to realize we're still at
          war.
                         (MORE)

                                                              (CONTINUED)

> BILL SULLIVAN (CONT'D)
> It's just a different kind of war with
> different enemies...And with the bomb
> the world's an even more dangerous
> place. I think it was a mistake
> disbanding OSS. I've been telling the
> president about the need to create a
> new Foreign Intelligence Service... to
> do in peacetime what OSS did during
> the war...It would be limited to
> overseas -- subversive operations...
> intelligence gathering and analysis...
> I'd be interested to know some of your
> thoughts -- particularly in your area
> of expertise... counterintelligence.

> EDWARD
> I'll be glad to help in any way I can,
> sir. (noticing his son) Edward, go
> outside...Margaret!

> CLOVER
> Let's go back outside. Your father is
> busy. (to the men) I'm sorry.

The General's quiet, and he looks old, out of his time...

> BILL SULLIVAN
> I have to tell you Edward, despite how
> much we need it, I have some real
> problems with this whole thing...I'm
> concerned that too much power will end
> up in the hands of too few. It's
> always in somebody's best interest to
> promote enemies... real or imagined...

Edward is quiet.

> BILL SULLIVAN (CONT'D)
> ...I see this as America's eyes and
> ears... I don't want it to become its
> heart and soul...

Edward doesn't say anything.

> BILL SULLIVAN (CONT'D)
> I told the President for this to work
> there's going to have to be some kind
> of civilian oversight...

> EDWARD
> Oversight?! How can you have a covert
> organization if someone's looking over
> your shoulder?

> BILL SULLIVAN
> Do you know who gave Hitler his
> power...? The clerks and the
> bookkeepers... the civil servants... I
> have this one weakness, Edward... I
> believe in a just God... I always seem
> to err on the side of democracy...

As they sit in the gathering darkness talking, Edward Jr.
talks to himself, pretend Army:

95   EXT. 1947, EDWARD'S SUBURBAN HOUSE, ALEXANDRIA - NIGHTFALL 95

Edward and Sullivan come out of house. The Redhaired Man crosses to a car. Sullivan slows and looks around, Clover still talking to the women on the lawn...

> BILL SULLIVAN
> This must be a nice place to raise a family... I never made the time... I'll be dead in less than a year... (as if passing the mantel, fearful) I love this country...

> EDWARD
> We all do, sir. We all do.

The General nods. He looks at Edward.

> BILL SULLIVAN
> Be very careful, Edward. No matter what anybody tells you, there will be no one you can trust.

They look at each other. Turning, hobbling on his wooden crutches, he crosses to his car, then slows...

> BILL SULLIVAN (CONT'D)
> I'm afraid when all is said and done, we're all just clerks too...

Edward watches him drive away, he sees Edward Jr. sitting on the curb, watching the other boys play catch with their fathers. Edward Jr. turns and they look at each other...

96   OMITTED SCENES 96-100   96

101   INT. 1947, CIA MEETING ROOM, WASHINGTON D.C. - DAY   101

We see a conference room with eight chairs on each side of a mahogany table. Six men are seated at the table, all in their 40s or 50s, the "Barons" of the CIA. Also present are Edward, Hayes, and Philip Allen.

The lights have been dimmed, and a FILM plays on a screen, highlighting a Central American leader, DR. IBANEZ, nationalizing property, growing in popularity...

> RICHARD HAYES
> ...He's nationalized over thirty percent of the land... all of it appropriated from our interests down there...

> EDWARD
> I was under the impression Dr. Ibanez supported democracy...

> PHILIP ALLEN
> I'm afraid he's changed his mind.

(CONTINUED)

                    RICHARD HAYES
          The doctor's started to believe his own
          propaganda -- I mean you dreamed this
          guy up, Edward -- helped get him
          elected... All that horseshit -- "El
          Indio --" "A man of the people..."
          "The Great Healer." Shit, it isn't very
          hard, they probably have ten doctors in
          the whole fucking country...

                    EDWARD
          One hundred and three...

He turns back to the film, which shows Dr. Ibanez speaking to a
large crowd. Near him, is the Soviet Foreign Minister, Molotov.

                    PHILIP ALLEN
          Those are the Soviets...Foreign
          Minister Molotov. Next to him is Trade
          Minister Trubnikov. The Soviets have
          become overly interested in their
          natural resources. Particularly
          coffee.

                    EDWARD
          Can you stop? Go back a little...Run
          it from there.

Edward looks at somebody. We can see, indistinctly, Stas, in
the background...

                    EDWARD (CONT'D)
          It's nothing. I thought I saw
          something.

As Edward walks back, Philip turns to him, lighting his pipe:

                    PHILIP ALLEN
          That's all. I'd like you and Mr. Hayes
          to put your heads together on the
          Central America account...I'm
          concerned about the Soviet presence.

Edwards nods quietly...From a set of chairs lined up against
the wall, a younger fair-haired MAN comes beside them:
MICHAEL JOHNSON.

                    RICHARD HAYES
          Michael's going down there with The
          Mayan Coffee Company as an
          "Agricultural Specialist." He'll be
          our eyes and ears...

Edward, his business done, starts to leave...

                    EDWARD
          Good luck...You might not want to wear
          that "ring" down there...

                    MICHAEL JOHNSON
          Of course. Thanks.

101   CONTINUED: (2)   101

Michael looks at his "Yale" class Ring. He nods. Edward
leaves, looking back, seeing Allen and Hayes talking. He
READS Allen's lips:

                    PHILIP ALLEN
          "I want all intelligence on this sent
          directly to me and no one else."

102   EXT. 1947 EDWARD'S SUBURBAN STREET,VIRGINIA - EARLY EVENING 102

Edward in raincoat, with briefcase, coming home. He sees
Clover, drink in hand, talking with a woman. Edward Jr. plays
with other boys. A Taxi stops. Clovers' mouth drops...Edward
turns. Standing in the street, in Army uniform, JOHN RUSSELL.
Clover runs to him, holding him to make sure he's real.
Edward, as startled as anyone, comes into the street...

                    EDWARD
          John?

                    JOHN RUSSELL
          Hello Edward.

They embrace, "the boys of summer." Edward realizes a Woman
is standing near him, a young dark haired pregnant woman.

                    JOHN RUSSELL (CONT'D)
          My sister Clover. Edward... This is my
          wife, Irina...

                    EDWARD
          Hello.

And as Clover introduces Edward Jr. to her brother...

103   EXT. 1947, EDWARD SUBURBAN HOUSE, BACK PORCH - NIGHT   103

Edward and John sit on back porch quietly talking privately.
Through the back window, Irina and Clover talk inside...

                    EDWARD
          She can't hear you, John.

                    JOHN RUSSELL
          ...Fifty miles from Peking... The
          Japanese Koyushu Prisoner of War Camp.

Tears well up from the memories... Regaining his composure:

                    JOHN RUSSELL (CONT'D)
          ...I was "freed" by the Russians in
          March of 1945... They detained me as an
          "undesirable," an American agent, and
          put me in the State Hospital in
          Novgorod...Irina was a nurse there.
          They had me teach English at a school
          there. I was part of a diplomatic
          exchange a month ago... Army
          Intelligence has been debriefing me
          since... (after a beat) My father had a
          conversation with Mr. Allen.
                    (MORE)

103   CONTINUED: 103
                        JOHN RUSSELL (CONT'D)
                Mr. Allen thought I might be able to
                help with identifying people who were
                so "interested" in learning to speak
                English there. The KGB called it a
                "charm school." I've been asked to work
                with your people... On the Soviet desk.

        Edward is silent. And as they sit on the back porch...

                        EDWARD
                We'll see what we can do.

104   INT. 1947, EDWARD'S HOUSE, ALEXANDRIA - NIGHT, LATER   104

        Edward and Clover see John and Irina out. John shrugs on his
        overcoat. An awkward moment. They look at each other. John
        embraces him. Clover kisses Irina, and holds her brother. John
        and Irina head off in a taxi. Edward shuts the door.

                        EDWARD
                It is good to see him again.

        Clover folds her arms across her chest as if she were chilled.

                        CLOVER
                I don't know why I'm afraid, Edward.

        And in a moment of affection he holds her.

                        EDWARD
                There's nothing to be afraid of. It's
                wonderful to have him home.

        She nods. They're quiet. She looks at him.

                        CLOVER
                Would you come up to bed with me?

                        EDWARD
                Would you like me to?

                        CLOVER
                I would like that.

        He goes up with her to the dark at the top of the stairs...

105   INT. 1947, EDWARD'S SUBURBAN HOUSE, BEDROOM - NIGHT, LATER 105

        Edward and Clover lie in bed in the dark bedroom...Clover is
        sleeping, clutching Edward's hand. He watches her sleep...He
        unclasps her hand and gets out of bed, trying not to wake her.

A106   INT. EDWARD'S HOUSE, STUDY - NIGHT   A106

        Edward plugs his phone into the wall jack, dialing...

                        EDWARD
                This is Carlson, GH-71. I want "a deep
                water" done, an all source trace from
                every agency in the community on
                following IDENS...

                                                      (CONTINUED)

He hangs up. A few moments, and the ringer on the study wall rings, blinking. Edward plugs the phone into a second jack and picks up, continuing the conversation.

>   EDWARD (CONT'D)
>   ...IDEN A., Russell, John A...D.P.O.B,
>   March 22, 1917, New Canaan,
>   Connecticut...IDEN B., Zaitseva,
>   Irena, accompanied Russell to U.S.,
>   arrival date, 9/18, from Moscow...
>   Check INS.

He hangs up. He senses somebody watching him. He turns and his son, in his pajamas, stands in the study door.

>   EDWARD (CONT'D)
>   Come back to bed.

>   EDWARD JR.
>   What were you talking about, father?

>   EDWARD
>   It's grownup talk. Go back to sleep.
>   You don't want to be tired for school
>   tomorrow.

>   EDWARD JR.
>   I had a nightmare.

>   EDWARD
>   Everything's fine... come back to bed.

He takes him back to his bedroom. As he gets into bed...

>   EDWARD JR.
>   We went to the Smithsonian. Look what
>   I got.

He opens a night stand drawer and shows him a snow globe of the Capital Building. Edward shakes it, quietly watching the snow. He puts it down next to Dickens' "A Christmas Carol."

>   EDWARD
>   Go to bed.

>   EDWARD JR.
>   Could you stay with me another minute?

He turns and sees his ringer blinking in the Study.

>   EDWARD
>   Try to go back to sleep.

He goes out, heading to the study. The boy's door opens. Edward Jr., from his own door, looking into Edward' Study. He hears his father talking on the phone, secretive, bits and pieces of his muffled conversation...

>   EDWARD'S VOICE
>   Keep the Bureau out of it...They can't
>   be trusted.
>   (MORE)

A106   CONTINUED: (2)   A106

                          EDWARD'S VOICE (CONT'D)
               We'll Keep it in the family for
               now...Wherever it leads us, we'll take
               care of our own... Mr. Russell, yes,
               he's my brother in law...No, I don't
               want anything done differently. No
               velvet gloves..If he's one of their's
               he's just as much a traitor...I don't
               want him having anything above a Level B
               Clearance--and I want Mosconi doing the
               polygraph...

          And as Edward Jr. listens to his father on the phone...

106   INT. 1947, EDWARD'S OFFICE, THE CIA - DAY   106

          Edward at desk, immersed in some FILES on KGB officers. In
          particular, a file on Stas Siyanko...Edward's Secretary enters
          with a small gift-wrapped package...

                          SECRETARY
               This just came for you through the
               Carlson Cover Address. There was no
               name.

                          EDWARD
                       (doesn't look up, to Ray)
               Open it?

          Ray unwraps it. Inside is a CAN OF COFFEE.

                          EDWARD (CONT'D)
                       (looks)
               Open it up...

          Ray takes the "key" and opens the can slowly. It hisses...

                          EDWARD (CONT'D)
               Look inside it.

          Ray feels inside. He stops, and drops a man's FINGER on desk
          with a YALE RING. Edward is still. He Knows where it came from.

107   INT. 1947, A COFFEE SHOP, WASHINGTON - DAY   107

          Edward eats some pie with coffee. A Man comes to his booth,
          and gives him a paper bag.

                          THE MAN
               I think this is what you are looking
               for. They're quite dependable.

          The Man leaves. Edward pulls a small JAR with a WINGED INSECT
          out of the bag, then puts it back in bag.

A108   INT. 1947, A CITY BUS - EVENING   A108

          Edward, in overcoat, briefcase at his side, riding home... The
          bus stops and people get on and off...It pulls away. A figure
          sits beside him. Edward turns and sees SAM MURACH, smoking.

                                                          (CONTINUED)

> SAM MURACH
> You look good, Edward. How many years
> is it? Eight? Nine years. Lot of water
> under the bridge...

Edward is quiet. As they ride...

> SAM MURACH (CONT'D)
> Carolyn and I, we just bought our
> first house...and everything's already
> broken...I spend my weekends fixing
> things...By the time I get everything
> fixed, it'll be time to sell the
> fucking house...

He smiles at life's vagaries. After some moments:

> EDWARD
> What's on your mind? You didn't come
> for a bus ride?

> SAM MURACH
> The Director's worried about the way
> the country's been going. Some people
> are saying, we wait to long, there'll
> be a commie under every bed. I'm
> hoping we can find a way to work
> together again... It would benefit
> both agencies... After all, last I
> looked, we work for the same country.

> EDWARD
> You know our charter prohibits us from
> doing anything on our soil.

> SAM MURACH
> Yeah, I know... And the first time you
> boys have the opportunity, you'll be
> breaking and entering, like thieves in
> the night, in deepest, darkest, Indiana.

Even Edward smiles. They're quiet...After some moments...

> EDWARD
> What about the wedge between us?

> SAM MURACH
> We'll never trust each other. FBI are
> working stiffs. CIA, you guys over
> there don't want to share a bathroom
> with me...But you and me are
> different. We have a special
> relationship.

The bus comes to a stop.

> SAM MURACH (CONT'D)
> It was good to see you again.

He gets up to go. Edward stops him.

> EDWARD
> Maybe you could give me a "heads up"
> on a couple of people.

He writes two names on a piece of paper, giving it to Sam.

> SAM MURACH
> You're asking me to give you FBI files
> on American citizens? You know I
> can't do that. It's against the law to
> spy on citizens...

> EDWARD
> What did you once say... "Spying is
> what other people do to us..."

They look at each other...

> SAM MURACH
> Let's keep in touch.

Sam exits bus, and it pulls away...Edward watches him go..

108   EXT. 1947, A COFFEE PLANTATION, CENTRAL AMERICA - DAY   108

Workers on a hillside, bent over working. Some CARS. In the
OFFICIAL CAR is Dr. Ibanez, two aides, and Stas. The cars
stop, they get out. Dr. Ibanez shows Stas the success of
nationalism...He moves to a small podium to speak to the
workers...

> DR. IBANEZ
> (In Spanish)
> "This coffee plantation shows that
> when people collectively work
> together, the result is a better and
> more productive society. This is our
> patriotic wish to advance, to
> progress, to win economic independence
> to match our political independence…
> One day the obscured forces which
> today oppress the backward and
> colonial world will be defeated. With
> the satisfaction of one who believes
> he has done his duty, with faith in
> the future, I say to you: Long live
> the October revolution! Long live our
> beloved country!"

The distant drone of an AIRPLANE. They look up at the gray
sky, the plane above the clouds... A breeze ruffles their
clothing. A small winged INSECT lands on a worker's shoulder.
He brushes it off. It's oddly quiet. Then more winged
insects, falling from sky. They eat away at the coffee
plants, destroying Dr. Ibanez' crops...

109   EXT. 1947, PHILIP ALLEN'S HOUSE, WASHINGTON D.C. - NIGHT 109

An elegant red brick home. Clover, Edward and Edward Jr. get
out of their car. As they approach entrance...

(CONTINUED)

109   CONTINUED: 109

                         CLOVER
                    (to Edward Jr.)
               Don't touch anything...

Edward rings the bell. Philip Allen answers the door...

                         PHILIP ALLEN
               Well, hello... I'm so glad to see you
               could come. Come in. Come in. (to
               Edward Jr.) You must be Edward. We
               have a very special guest for you
               tonight.

                         CLOVER
                    (to her son)
               Take off your hat.

110   INT. 1947, PHILIP ALLEN'S HOUSE, WASHINGTON D.C. - NIGHT 110

His faceless wife Toddy, comes over to greet them.

                         PHILIP ALLEN
               You know Toddy.

                         EDWARD
               This is Edward. Say hello to Mr. and
               Mrs. Allen.

Politely, he does.

                         PHILIP ALLEN
               Since Toddy and I never had the
               opportunity to have children of our
               own we particularly enjoy having the
               children over...

He leads them into a living room with a large Christmas tree
where some children waiting for their turn is SANTA CLAUS.

                         CLOVER
               Look, Santa Claus...

Edward Jr. quietly stands at his mother's side.

                         CLOVER (CONT'D)
                    (smiles at Toddy)
               He's scared to death of Santa...

She takes him by the hand...

                         CLOVER (CONT'D)
               Come darling, you'll enjoy it.

He shakes "no."

                         TODDY ALLEN
                    (offers her hand)
               Why don't you come with me...?

He has no choice. He reluctantly takes her hand, walking off.

                                              (CONTINUED)

                         PHILIP ALLEN
              Toddy's wonderful with children.
              Would you like a drink, Edward?

Edward follows him into a STUDY with Men from the CIA. Among
them, Richard Hayes, and in wheelchair, the terminally ill,
emaciated, Bill Sullivan.

                         PHILIP ALLEN (CONT'D)
                    (aside to Edward)
              You know he lost his leg.

Edward nods, and Philip brings him a drink.

                         BILL SULLIVAN
              You can be very proud of what you men
              in this room have started. To CIA.

They drink to that.

                         BILL SULLIVAN (CONT'D)
              Now let's get drunk.

They laugh. As people drink, Edward stands by Sullivan. He looks
out the door... He can see his son nearing Santa Claus. Their
eyes meet, the little boy scared to death. Edward subtly gives
him his approval, then turns back to the study. He looks back at
his son and sees him petrified, on Santa's lap, urine dripping
down his leg. Clover grabs him off Santa and Edward rushes over.

                         CLOVER
              What's the matter with you...!?

                         EDWARD JR.
                    (crying)
              I'm sorry... I couldn't help it...

Clover looks in the study...

                         CLOVER
              Edward, I think we should go home...

                         EDWARD
              Lower your voice...(to Edward Jr.)
              It's alright.

                         TODDY ALLEN
                    (coming over)
              You can use our bath if you'd like...
              I might have some dry clothes... My
              nephew's...

As he takes his son upstairs...

111   INT. 1947, THE BATHROOM, PHILIP ALLEN'S HOUSE - NIGHT   111

He undresses him. His son puts his arms around Edward's neck,
hugging him, pressing his cheek to his father's.

                         EDWARD JR.
              I'm sorry.

                                                    (CONTINUED)

CONTINUED:

                              EDWARD
                    It's okay.

And he helps him into the shower as WE HEAR VOICES SINGING...

112   INT. 1947, THE LIVING ROOM, PHILIP ALLEN'S - NIGHT, LATER 112

Everyone is by the Christmas Tree. Toddy plays Christmas carols
on piano as people sing: "O come, all ye faithful, joyful and
triumphant... O come ye, O come ye, to Bethlehem..."

113   INT. 1947, PRESIDENTIAL PALACE, CENTRAL AMERICA - NIGHT   113

DR. IBANEZ and family sit around a Christmas tree opening
gifts. A door opens. Two Soldiers burst in, followed by Ten
others, leveling their weapons. Some soldiers grab Dr.
Ibanez, manhandling him, and pull him from the room...

114   INT. 1947, THE LIVING ROOM, PHILIP ALLEN'S HOUSE - NIGHT 114

Hayes comes in, whispers to Allen. He nods, and goes to Edward.

                         PHILIP ALLEN
                 The Doctor has no more patients...

Edward doesn't say anything. As Philip Allen sings...

                         BILL SULLIVAN
                      (quietly to Edward)
                 Did you know that Mr. Allen is going
                 to be on the Central American Coffee
                 Company Board of Directors...?
                 Remember what I said to you about
                 friends?

Edward looks at Allen, who tamps pipe, lighting it, as all
continue to SING "Oh come all ye faithful..."

115   INT. 1961, EDWARD'S OFFICE, THE CIA - DAY   115

"Saturday, April 22, 1961." We see big letters through a
magnifying glass: FROIDE. Edward, a shadow of himself,
looking at a BLOWUP of the fan's brand plate.

                    TECHNICAL OFFICER # 2
                 The fan...We were able to make out the
                 brand. It's a "Froide." It's made in
                 Belgium...

Edward then moves to the BLOW UP of the object on the night
stand, an Abstract Painting.

                    TECHNICAL OFFICER # 2 (CONT'D)
                 The object on the night stand, we're
                 still trying to find out what this is.
                 We just can't get any more definition
                 out of it...

Edward dismisses the Technical Officer. And as he peers into
the shadows...That could just as well be his life...

116   INT. 1953, EDWARD'S SUBURBAN HOUSE, DINING ROOM - NIGHT   116

Edward and Clover, just done with dinner with their NEIGHBORS.
Clover has barely touched her food, drinking dinner instead.

                    THE YOUNG MAN
          ...Margaret tells us that you work for
          the CIA...

                    EDWARD
          My wife has a vivid imagination. I'm
          just a trade adviser... A civil
          servant...   (a smile) Clover likes to
          sometimes exaggerate.

There's silence as they continue to eat, finishing...And
their guests awkwardly get up, talking about how "You must
come to our house next time..."

117   INT. 1953, EDWARD'S SUBURBAN HOUSE, LIVING ROOM - NIGHT   117

Edward and Clover in the living room.

                    CLOVER
          You had no right to talk to me that
          way...! Those people are my friends...!
          I don't have a lot of friends.

She starts into the kitchen. Edward stops her, chilling:

                    EDWARD
          You are never to tell anyone what I
          do! Do you understand that? Never.

                    CLOVER
          What you do?! I don't know what you
          do! I don't know anything about you!
          You leave at five and you're home at
          ten... seven days a week... You
          haven't said two words to me in a
          month... I feel like I'm living with a
          ghost...

Tears run down her cheeks. The PHONE RINGS. Edward picks up.

                    A MAN'S VOICE (OVER)
          Mr. Carlson, please.

                    EDWARD
          Call back on two.

He hangs up. He disconnects the phone from the wall jack,
connects it into another jack. He dials. After five RINGS...

                    RAY BROCCO'S VOICE (OVER)
          We have somebody taking a swim.

Edward hangs up.

                    EDWARD
          I have to go out...

                                        (CONTINUED)

STILLS

Matt Damon as Edward Wilson and Robert De Niro as Bill Sullivan.

Angelina Jolie as Clover with Matt Damon as Edward.

Robert De Niro directs Matt Damon.

Robert De Niro directs Matt Damon.

Matt Damon as Edward Wilson in his office.

Robert De Niro with Matt Damon.

Angelina Jolie as Margaret Wilson.

Matt Damon as Edward Wilson consoling Angelina Jolie as his distraught wife.

Robert De Niro as Bill Sullivan at Edward Wilson's home.

Angelina Jolie as Margaret waiting out another
interruption as Edward takes a call.

Margaret with her son

Edward Wilson at home.

Robert De Niro directs Angelina Jolie and Matt Damon.

Robert De Niro at work directing.

Robert De Niro directs Angelina Jolie.

Robert De Niro directs Angelina Jolie.

Robert De Niro directs Angelina Jolie and Matt Damon.

Matt Damon as Edward Wilson.

The director at work.

The director and star on the set.

Eric Roth, the screenwriter, with Robert De Niro.

Robert De Niro with Eric Roth, the screenwriter.

The director at work.

117   CONTINUED:

He goes into foyer to get his coat.

                    CLOVER
          I'm sorry...Say something! Say
          something!

                    EDWARD JR.'S VOICE
          Mother. Father.

They see Edward Jr., 13, standing at the foot of stairs.
Clover runs off into the Kitchen as Edward looks at him...

                    EDWARD
          I have to go out. Please keep an eye
          on your mother. She isn't feeling
          well.

Edward Jr. nods. Edward seems about to say something personal,
but he can't, and buttoning his coat starts to leave. Edward
Jr. stands there quietly, Clover in kitchen, pouring herself
another drink...Edward Jr. going into the kitchen...

                    EDWARD JR.
               (concerned, protecting her)
          How was your night, mother? Are you
          alright?

                    CLOVER
          I'm fine sweetheart...Were we too
          loud...Did we wake you up?

                    EDWARD JR.
          Father has to go out. I just thought
          you might want some company.

                    CLOVER
               (desperate for company)
          I'd love your company. Can I make you
          some hot chocolate?

He sits at the kitchen table, keeping his mother company as
Edward goes out the door into the night.

118   INT. HALLWAY, THE CIA - NIGHT   118

Edward and Ray and an Operations Officers walk down a hall...

                    OPERATIONS OFFICER # 1
               (reading a cable)
          ...At 22:42 call received on Berlin
          base chief's operational line. Man
          says he is senior officer, Line KR,
          KGB. Would not give name. Demanded
          Chief of Base Berlin establish
          immediate link with Mr. Edward Wilson
          and present following demands... An
          American sedan with red U.S. Army
          plates be in front of Gedaechtnis
          Kirche and proceed directly to
          Templehof Air Base where dedicated
          aircraft will wait to bring him to
          Andrews Air Force Base.
                    (MORE)

                                        (CONTINUED)

118   CONTINUED: 118

                              OPERATIONS OFFICER # 1 (CONT'D)
                    When airborne and Mr. Wilson satisfies
                    these needs, he will identify himself.

A119   INT. 1953, OLD COMMUNICATIONS ROOM, THE CIA - NIGHT   A119

As they enter the Communications center, we hear chatter
inside. A communication officer turns toward them:

                              COMMUNICATIONS OFFICER
                         (reading to them)
                    KGB officer asks when Mr. Edward
                    Wilson coming. Why is it taking him so
                    long? He wants to know Mr. Edward
                    Wilson's response.

                              EDWARD
                    Tell him Mr. Edward Wilson is here and
                    would like to know what he intends to
                    provide in return.

He types in response. They wait, then the machine chatters...

                              COMMUNICATIONS OFFICER # 1
                    KGB officer laughed that Mr. Wilson
                    asks such rudimentary question.

                              RAY BROCCO
                    He's pretty sure of himself.

                              EDWARD
                    Tell him, "Mr. Wilson doesn't deal
                    with people who just want to hear
                    themselves talk."

The officer types... And they wait... The machine chatters...

                              COMMUNICATIONS OFFICER # 1
                    He responded; tell Mr. Wilson, "What
                    is it you Americans say, talk is not
                    cheap..."

Edward slightly smiles...The machine chatters again...

                              RAY BROCCO
                    He says in return for safe journey, he
                    will provide Mr. Wilson with clear
                    understanding of last three loses in
                    Moscow...penetrations at Moscow
                    station...and identities of Soviet
                    agents in your country... he will also
                    speak personally and very privately
                    with Mr. Edward Wilson about Ulysses.

At the mention of "Ulysses," Edward looks up.

                              RAY BROCCO (CONT'D)
                    Things only he knows of Ulysses; how
                    he thinks, what he plans to do, and
                    what he wants Mr. Edward Wilson to
                    think he is doing...(a beat) To
                    establish bonafides, will carry with
                    him KGB surveillance photographs of
                    all CIA officers in Moscow...
                              (MORE)   (CONTINUED)

CONTINUED:

                         RAY BROCCO (CONT'D)
               and would be more than happy to take
               polygraph.

The machine is momentarily silent. And then the chattering...

                         RAY BROCCO (CONT'D)
               "Tell me, Mr. Wilson, is talk still
               cheap?"

                         EDWARD
               Tell him, before I give him anything,
               who am I dealing with? What is his
               name?

The machine types back a response...

                         RAY BROCCO
               Mr. Wilson, I was not born another
               day. When I am coming safely to you--I
               will tell you who I am.

Edward is quiet, thinking.

                         EDWARD
               Ulysses. (a beat) What is his
               weakness?

There's an extended silence. They wait. And then the teletype
chatters..."THE COLD."

                         EDWARD (CONT'D)
               Let's get him a plane.

Ray goes to a phone...

                         RAY BROCCO
               Air Branch, please.

119   INT. 1953, A SAFE HOUSE, A ROOM NEXT DOOR, MARYLAND - DAY 119

       Edward, with headphones, looks at his KGB FILE on Valentin,
       codename, "Concerto." Inside is a PHOTO of a group of men in
       swimsuits on a boat on a Russian lake. Valentin has purposely
       moved so he is out of focus. Edward looks down at photo with a
       magnifying glass, then up through a two-way mirror at Valentin
       on a couch in a living room, dark haired and relaxed. It's
       impossible to tell if the man in the photo and the man on the
       couch are the same. Next to Edward, are two Technical Officers
       monitoring two reel to reel players, and a frumpy older woman,
       a Soviet expert, taking notes, passing notes on a 3x5 INDEX
       CARD during the debriefing. As Edward peers out at Valentin:

120   INT. 1953, THE SAFE HOUSE, MARYLAND - DAY   120

       Across from Valentin is Ray Brocco in a chair, looking at a
       dossier, and a Case Officer on a bridge chair in dining room.

                         VALENTIN
               My name is Valentin Gregorieviich
               Mironov. My children's names are
               Anitoly and Sergei... My father played
               the cello... I play the violin...But
               you know this.
                         (MORE)

                                                      (CONTINUED)

120   CONTINUED: 120

                         VALENTIN (CONT'D)
               (annoyed) I risk my life to come all
               the way to tell you this... To confirm
               what you already know...?

                         RAY BROCCO
               You failed the polygraph, Mr. Mironov.

                         VALENTIN
               You know every Russian fails
               polygraph. Your polygraph doesn't
               understand Russian soul. What more do
               you want? I've given you my bonafides.
               The names and identities of agents.
               Who has been compromised in Moscow.
               Who you need to know about...

                         RAY BROCCO
               Your immediate superior was who?

                         VALENTIN
                    (frustrated)
               I told you this three times already.
               Sergei Budanov. (demands) I would like
               some tea.

Ray nods. The young Case Officer goes into the kitchen and
goes through the spare shelves. There's no tea.

                         RAY BROCCO
               There isn't any.

                         VALENTIN
               I would like you to make me some hot
               water with lemon then. I get thirsty
               when I sit too much. (and to Ray) Are
               you going to keep up this inane
               questioning up for much longer?

A121   INT. 1953, THE SAFE HOUSE, A ROOM NEXT DOOR - DAY   A121

Edward watches Valentin and Bracco through two-way mirror.
Ray gets up, crossing to stand by Valentin.

                         RAY BROCCO
               There's nothing you've told us we
               don't know, Mr. Mironov... I think you
               better try a little harder.

                         VALENTIN
               I didn't come here to deal with
               children Mr. Jones...Or is it Mr.
               Brocco... (arrogant) We do our
               homework too...I told you I want to
               speak to Mr. Wilson.

                         RAY BROCCO
               Is there something you would like to
               share with Mr. Wilson? I'll be glad
               to relay any information to him.

                         VALENTIN
               Yes, you can tell Mr. Edward Wilson...

And he turns directly to the two way mirror...

                                                    (CONTINUED)

CONTINUED:

                         VALENTIN'S VOICE
                    You give a child medicine, how do you
                    say it, "a spoonful at a time..."

121   EXT. 1953, THE SAFE HOUSE, WASHINGTON - DUSK   121

Valentin looks out at the Potomac. Ray and two Security
Officers stand nearby talking. Edward comes over to Valentin.

                         EDWARD
                    Mr. Mironov... I'm Mr. Carlson, I
                    represent Mr. Wilson...

They shake hands. They're quiet, looking at the river. A cold
breeze blows off the water. Valentin recites to him:

                         VALENTIN
                    "One day, when childhood tumbled the
                    spongy tufts, Banking the naked edge
                    of our bottom lands, A shadowy crane
                    arose with a flipping fish, A speckled
                    rainbow, Speared in her slim black
                    bill..."

                         EDWARD
                    "...Under that dark ark, Two grappling
                    anchors of dangling legs Rolled away so
                    smoothly the eye forgot them Until that
                    tall, ungainly crane lay in the sky
                    like a dream..." Fyodor Nesteranko.

                         VALENTIN
                    I didn't know what you looked like.
                    Hello, "Mother."

                         EDWARD
                    What brings you to us, Mr. Mironov?

                         VALENTIN
                    I want to see the sky.

122   OMITTED   122

123   INT. 1953, TRAIN STATION, WASHINGTON, D.C. - NIGHT   123

Edward enters a busy TRAIN STATION. He sees Sam Murach, smoking.

                         EDWARD
                    What's on your mind?

                         SAM MURACH
                    I want to show you something.

And while they move into position on the mezzanine stairs...

                         SAM MURACH (CONT'D)
                    Carolyn won a teaching award...Now
                    I've got to rent a tuxedo for the
                    banquet...

And he turns, seeing someone coming...Edward slows. He sees
JOHN RUSSELL, carrying a newspaper, coming into the terminal.
                                                     (CONTINUED)

> SAM MURACH (CONT'D)
> He's been coming here once a month for
> the last three months... making dead
> drops...We're guessing microfilm.
> We've been watching him since we were
> told he failed his polygraph with you.

John turns to a phone booth, seemingly using the phone...
then walks off, his newspaper left behind. A moment, and a
gray haired MAN goes into John's booth. He comes out with the
newspaper, crossing to another exit. Edward is quiet.

> SAM MURACH (CONT'D)
> That gray haired guy is Boris
> Levchenko, stationed at the Russian
> Embassy...Do you want us to stop him?

> EDWARD
> (shaking his head 'no')
> No. We take care of our own.

Sam gives a signal to one of his guys to let them go. And
with that, a man on a bench gets up, puts his coat on, and
walks out. A few moments, and then another man goes out in
another direction. Then a few moments later, another man goes
out another direction.

> SAM MURACH
> (genuinely)
> I'm sorry, Edward...Even in the "best"
> of families... (beat) It was good to
> see you again.

Sam puts on his hat and goes down the stairs. As Edward looks
out at the station below...

124   EXT. 1953, EDWARD'S SUBURBAN HOUSE, FRONT YARD - DAY   124

A snowy winter day. Edward's and John's families come out of
Edward's home as they walk to John's car...

> JOHN RUSSELL
> It's nice to have the families together.

Edward nods...

> JOHN RUSSELL (CONT'D)
> Moments like these, it's as if the
> world doesn't exist.

> EDWARD
> It all goes too quickly. We were just
> boys ourselves.

They look at each other, not boys anymore... And Edward says:

> EDWARD (CONT'D)
> I was at the train station, John...

(CONTINUED)

>   JOHN RUSSELL
>   I know. I was told. The FBI's been
>   watching me for weeks. That's the way
>   it was supposed to play out.

John looks at him.   There are tears in his pale blue eyes...

>   JOHN RUSSELL (CONT'D)
>   They want me to hide in plain sight,
>   Edward... They want me to go out into
>   the cold...

>   EDWARD
>   I didn't hear that? On whose direction?

>   JOHN RUSSELL
>   You know I can't tell you that.
>   You're not in the compartment...You
>   don't need to know. (quietly)
>   I'm on a stand alone... All alone...
>   Trust me, Edward. I love my country.
>   I'm doing this for my country...

>   IRINA
>   John?

>   EDWARD
>   I'll be right there.
>   (to Edward)
>   We're family, Edward... Please, I
>   need you to believe me...

Edward is quiet, not knowing what to believe. John goes to
his wife and child. Edward turns, seeing his son.

>   EDWARD JR.
>   Why was uncle John crying...?

>   EDWARD
>   He doesn't know who he is right now.

>   EDWARD JR.
>   Doesn't know who he is? How is that?

>   EDWARD
>   The world's a complicated place. Some
>   people lose their way.

>   EDWARD JR.
>   I wouldn't want to ever lose my way.

>   EDWARD
>   I'm here to make sure you don't.

He sees Clover, arms folded protectively, walking back to the
house, passing Edward without a word...

125   EXT. 1953, THE SAFE HOUSE - WASHINGTON D.C. - DAY   125

Edward sits in the backseat of a Car. A Driver stands by the
car door, waiting. VALENTIN comes outside. He gets into the
back with Edward, and before they're driven off...

126   INT. 1953, THE CAR - MORNING   126

                    EDWARD
          I brought you something...

Ray hands him a violin case from the front of the car.

                    EDWARD (CONT'D)
          You said you played...

                    VALENTIN
          That was very thoughtful of you...

                    EDWARD
          I'd like to hear you play some time.

                    VALENTIN
          I would enjoy that.

                    EDWARD
              (opening case)
          Would you play, now?

                    VALENTIN
          Now?

                    EDWARD
          There's no time like the present...

                    VALENTIN
          I haven't played in quite a long time.

Edward takes out the violin and hands it to him...Valentin
takes up the violin, then puts it back down.

                    VALENTIN (CONT'D)
          Perhaps another time...I don't feel
          like playing now.

                    RAY BROCCO
          We insist.

                    EDWARD
          I'm afraid, there won't be another
          time.

Valentin takes up violin. He hesitates, then plays beautifully.

                    VALENTIN
          You have to learn to trust me, Mother.

127   EXT. 1953, WOODS OUTSIDE OF WASHINGTON - DAY   127

Valentin walks with Edward through the woods by the Safe House.

                    VALENTIN
          ...Stas Siyanko is obsessed with you.
          Night and day, you are always on his
          mind... He would say, tell me about
          Mother.
                       (MORE)

127   CONTINUED: 127

>   VALENTIN (CONT'D)
>   I want to live in mother's skin.
>   (smiling) He has even taken up a
>   hobby.
>
>   EDWARD
>   What's that?
>
>   VALENTIN
>   He has become fascinated with ships in
>   bottles. Everybody should have a
>   hobby, don't you think so, Mother?

Edward is quiet. After some moments, equally obsessed...

>   EDWARD
>   What else can you tell me about him?
>
>   VALENTIN
>   He is very difficult because he is
>   willing to lose now so he can win
>   later. He trusts nobody. The joke is
>   he has no mirrors in his house so that
>   he can't even see himself...The only
>   one whom he lets close is his aide,
>   the Tartar...He is methodical, he
>   plans things years in advance...For
>   instance, you should know, he has
>   developed a "friendship" with a
>   certain neighbor of yours...a young
>   man he has high hopes for...
>
>   EDWARD
>   Is there anybody else? Does he have a
>   lover? A mistress?
>
>   VALENTIN
>   His work is his mistress...

And as we look at their backs from a distance, walking, they
almost seem like best friends...

>   EDWARD'S VOICE
>   What can you tell me about this young
>   man in Cuba...?

128   INT. 1953, EDWARD'S OFFICE, THE CIA - ANOTHER DAY   128

McCarthy on the TV, Edward working at his desk as Ray comes in.

>   RAY BROCCO
>   "...the violinist" is here.
>
>   EDWARD
>   Find him some space.
>
>   RAY BROCCO
>   He hasn't been given clearance yet.
>
>   EDWARD
>   He has my approval...(taking up some
>   files) Let him start with this.

Ray leaves...Edward reads reports... As his private door opens:

(CONTINUED)

                         EDWARD (CONT'D)
               Don't use that door --

Arch Cummings, coat over arm, stands at the door with an
"Escort." A heavy-set man standing nearby.

                         ESCORT
               I'm sorry, sir. He just walked right
               by.

                         ARCH CUMMINGS
               Only you would have a door marked "Not
               an Exit..." Hello, dear Mother... The
               Tailor said I could visit you
                    (meaning "Escort")
               ...with a guardian angel, of course.

Edward smiles. Glad to see him. He motions Arch to come in.

                         EDWARD
                    (dismissing escort)
               ...

The Escort nods and goes to wait in the hall...

                         ARCH CUMMINGS
               I'm sure you're up on the news... I'm
               going to run our station here.

                         EDWARD
               I was very happy to hear that.

                         ARCH CUMMINGS
               I brought you a little something.

He gives him a small object wrapped in brown paper.

                         EDWARD
               You never come empty handed.

                         ARCH CUMMINGS
               I was raised well. Open it.

Edward unwraps. Inside is a small, decent PAINTING of a river.

                         ARCH CUMMINGS (CONT'D)
               I did it myself. The painting of the
               river that wasn't there...You see,
               Edward, some things are real after
               all.

                         EDWARD
                    (taken, grateful)
               Now all I need is a fireplace to put
               it over...

Arch laughs. He can go along with that. He turns and looks at
McCarthy on the television, being challenged by a defense
lawyer, the tide turning against him...

                                                 (CONTINUED)

                    ARCH CUMMINGS
          It's good to see at least in America
          everyone has come to their senses.

                    EDWARD
          We're sensible people.

                    ARCH   CUMMINGS
          I understand you had a most interesting
          fish swim your way. Mr. Allen said it
          might be possible for me to speak with
          him...with you, of course, as chaperone.

Edward takes up the phone. He quietly says something.

                    ARCH CUMMINGS
          It will be nice to be closely working
          with you again.

                    ARCH CUMMINGS (CONT'D)
          I expect you to show me Washington.
          We can paint the town red together.

                    EDWARD
          Red, white and blue...

Valentin comes in...

                    ARCH CUMMINGS
          Mr. Mironov, Arch Cummings... It's a
          pleasure to meet you...

                    VALENTIN
          My pleasure...

                    ARCH CUMMINGS
          It's nice to have someone like you on
          our side of the street.

Arch lights a cigarette, offering the pack to everyone.

                    ARCH CUMMINGS (CONT'D)
          I thought you might enjoy this. I hope
          you haven't read it.

He gives him a BOOK.

                    ARCH CUMMINGS (CONT'D)
          It's a first edition of James Joyce's,
          "Ulysses."

                    VALENTIN
               (seemingly moved)
          Thank you. A lovely thought. It was
          banned of course. I wasn't able to
          read it. There is so much I would like
          to read.

                    ARCH CUMMINGS
          You have the freedom to read anything
          you want now. There is a new world for
          you to explore. Isn't that so, Mother?

                                        (CONTINUED)

128   CONTINUED: (3)   128

                          EDWARD
               A whole new world.

                          ARCH CUMMINGS
               For all of us. We are still hopeless
               romantics, aren't we Edward?

                          EDWARD
               Hopeless romantics.

129   EXT. 1953, RUSSIAN EMBASSY, WASHINGTON - EARLY MORNING   129

       A Car pulls to a stop in the empty street. Irina's driving,
       John in the front, their boy asleep in the back. A moment and
       John gets out. He looks in the car, at his wife, his son. He
       taps on the glass to wake his son. The boy sleepily looking
       out the window. John kisses his fingertips onto the glass,
       saying "goodbye." Irina tries not to cry. He turns and
       crosses to the Embassy Gate. He stops at the Guard Station. A
       moment, and the gates open. He hesitates, looks behind him,
       waves a sad goodbye, and goes onto the Embassy grounds.
       TARTAR comes out to meet him. They talk, and he follows the
       Tartar to a side door, going inside. The Embassy is still,
       peaceful. Finally, Irina has the strength to drive away. PAN
       from the Embassy to a BUILDING down the street.

A130   INT. 1953, OBSERVATION POST - DAY   A130

       Edward and Sam Murach watch the Embassy through binoculars...

                          SAM MURACH
               We can stop him right here. He'll
               never get out of the country.

       Edward, after a beat, shakes "no."

                          EDWARD
               No. Let him go.

                          SAM MURACH
               Is he one of ours or is he one of
               theirs?

                          EDWARD
               You know I wouldn't tell you that...
               even if I did know...

       And as Edward quietly lowers his binoculars...

130   INT. 1953, EDWARD'S SUBURBAN HOUSE, BEDROOM - NIGHT   130

       Edward comes into the room. Clover's figure, seemingly asleep
       in the bed. He starts to undress.

                          CLOVER
               Why didn't you protect him?

                          EDWARD
               I was a friend to him.

                          CLOVER
               You abandoned him...

                                                        (CONTINUED)

130   CONTINUED:

                              EDWARD
                    I was a friend to him. I protected
                    him. He abandoned me.

                              CLOVER
                    You don't know the meaning of
                    friendship.

                              EDWARD
                    I've made sure his wife and child are
                    taken care of.

                              CLOVER
                    He needed you...

                              EDWARD
                    ...There is nothing else I can do. He
                    made the decisions he made.

                              CLOVER
                    You left him all alone. You do that to
                    people. You isolate them. That's what
                    you do. You isolate them.

They stop, staring at each other...And as Edward walks off
into the bathroom...

                              EDWARD
                    I'm as lonely as you are.

A131   INT. 1961, EDWARD'S OFFICE, THE CIA - NIGHT - APRIL 22   A131

Edward, alone, bent over the BLOW UP, trying to see through
the grain. A slight sound, and he turns to see Philip Allen.

                              PHILIP ALLEN
                    May I come in?

Edward nods. He comes into the office.

                              EDWARD
                    How was the fishing?

                              PHILIP ALLEN
                    It was a bad year. The water is too
                    high... Did you turn on the chastity
                    belt?

Edward presses a button under his desk and picks up the phone.
We hear white static, and he nods to Allen. Ray comes in...
Seeing Allen, he excuses himself.

                              PHILIP ALLEN (CONT'D)
                    Do you know I have never been in your
                    office? (looking around) All the
                    safes. Filled with all the secrets.

                              EDWARD
                    Everybody has a secret to tell,
                    something to hide.

                                                        (CONTINUED)

>   PHILIP ALLEN
> I suppose so. I understand you wanted
> to personally give me the Operation
> Zapata list yourself. (wise) There
> isn't one is there?

>   EDWARD
>   (shakes "no")
> Some things are more secret than others.
> You know it was a silent operation.

>   PHILIP ALLEN
> It wasn't silent enough. I've been
> asked by the President to suggest who
> we no longer need with us. Who would
> you recommend, Edward?

>   EDWARD
> I serve at the pleasure of the
> director. Those are your decisions,
> Philip. I'm just a gatekeeper.

>   PHILIP ALLEN
>   (smiles at his modesty)
> Why is it that people like us Edward,
> people with privilege, choose to serve
> for nickels a day in a profession that
> makes us constantly look over our
> shoulders to see who's watching us?

>   EDWARD
> When are you going to make a decision?

>   PHILIP ALLEN
> A decision?

>   EDWARD
> Who to keep and who to cut loose?

>   PHILIP ALLEN
> I serve at the discretion of the
> President of the United States. I'll do
> what I think is best for the country.

He looks around the office one more time and starts to leave.

>   EDWARD
> Philip... Are you still getting
> chocolates from Switzerland?

>   PHILIP ALLEN
>   (shakes "no," smiles)
> I have to live with my sweet tooth.
> We all have to make sacrifices,
> Edward. You know... (and he talks more
> than sings) "We are poor little lambs
> who have lost our way...Baa, baa,
> baa..." Goodnight.

(CONTINUED)

And Philip Allen leaves...Edward looks down at his safe, his
"insurance policy" inside...He gets up, puts on his coat and
hat, ready to go...We see Bracco locking each and every
drawer and safe...Edward goes out the door and into the
hall... Bracco, finished locking up comes out, starting to
lock the door to their office suite...

> EDWARD
> You checked them all?

> RAY BROCCO
> Yes, sir.

Edward checks each safe to make sure it's locked...And
without another word Edward starts along the hall, Bracco at
his side...And as they walk off...

> RAY BROCCO (CONT'D)
> When are you going to learn to trust
> me, Mother?

> A YOUNG MAN'S VOICE (OVER)
> "All Russia is our orchard..."

131   INT. 1958, A LITTLE THEATRE, WASHINGTON D.C. - NIGHT   131

Edward, Valentin, and Arch watch a local production of "The
Cherry Orchard." Edward senses somebody looking at him. He
turns and sees at the end of his aisle, program in lap, hair
tied back, a handsome woman... LAURA. She smiles, mouthing,
"Edward." He doesn't acknowledge her, looking straight ahead.
She looks at him, confused and hurt, as he watches the play.

> EDWARD
> (to Valentin, Arch)
> I'm due at a meeting.

They nod. Edward gets up, crosses purposely past Laura. Their
eyes meet. Without a word, he exits. Laura's still. After a
moment, upset, she gets up and leaves.

132   EXT. 1958, THE LITTLE THEATER, WASHINGTON D.C. - NIGHT   132

Laura comes outside to an empty sidewalk, some taxis waiting
by the street. She starts to turn to leave when:

> TAXI DRIVER
> Are you Laura?

> LAURA
> What?

> TAXI DRIVER
> Are you Laura? I'm supposed to offer
> you a ride. Mr. Wilson sent me.

She hesitates for a moment, then gets in. As it pulls away...

133   INT. 1958, A BAR, IN VIRGINIA - NIGHT   133

A small quiet bar. Laura comes in, looks around the bar. She
feels a hand on her shoulder, Edward behind her...

(CONTINUED)

133   CONTINUED:

                              EDWARD
                    Hello Laura...

                              LAURA
                    Why all the mystery?

                              EDWARD
                    Believe me, you are better off if you
                    don't know.

She looks at him... his eyes old before their time...

                              LAURA
                    You're scaring me...

                              EDWARD
                    You're safe with me, Laura.

She looks at him, nods, trusting, and lets him walk her in:

134   INT. 1958, BAR IN VIRGINIA - NIGHT, LATER   134

Edward and Laura in the quiet bar at a corner table...

                              LAURA
                    Do you have children?

                              EDWARD
                    I have a boy...Edward Jr. Do you have
                    anybody?

                              LAURA
                    A cat.
                         (her smile)
                    We understand each other.

He smiles and it's a smile from the past, a boy's smile...

                              LAURA (CONT'D)
                    I've been teaching English for three
                    years... At Gallaudet... It's a college
                    for the deaf here in Washington.

                              EDWARD
                    That must be very rewarding...

An awkward quiet. She wants to ask him about his work, but
she knows she can't, and doesn't really want to know either.

                              LAURA
                    I have often imagined what my life
                    would have been like with you...

                              EDWARD
                    What did you imagine?

                              LAURA
                    I thought you might teach... Probably
                    poetry... I saw us living in a small
                    college town...

(CONTINUED)

CONTINUED:

He smiles at the thought. They're quiet, each with their own thoughts of what might have been.

> EDWARD
> Laura, watch... I haven't forgotten.

He looks over at a COUPLE talking... "reading" their lips...

> EDWARD (CONT'D)
> She said she has to be up early for work... she'd like to go home. He said, "just one more drink..."

Laura nods at his skill. But there's something not so clever about it, its purpose perverted. He's telling her, in his own way, what he does.

> LAURA
> You once said to me you were afraid your life was already planned for you. Did it work out...? Are you doing what you want to do, Edward?

> EDWARD
> Life has been full of surprises.

They're quiet. They look at each other, so many years later.

135   EXT. 1958, THE BAR, VIRGINIA - NIGHT   135

They come out. He walks her to a taxi. She starts to get in...

> LAURA
> You owe me a day at the beach.

He smiles. She gets in and he kisses her cheek, walking away... There's an aching feeling of something so incomplete.

> LAURA (CONT'D)
> Edward...

He sees Laura standing by the curb. They look at each other...

136   INT. 1958, LAURA'S APARTMENT, WASHINGTON D.C. - NIGHT   136

Down a hall, an open bedroom door, Edward and Laura making love.

A137   INT. 1958, DEER ISLAND, EDWARD'S CABIN - NIGHT   A137

Clover, sitting at a dresser mirror, drink at her elbow, and not her first. Edward comes out of the dressing room...

> EDWARD
> How long do you think you'll be?

> CLOVER
> As long as it takes.

> EDWARD
> I'll go ahead then...

(CONTINUED)

                         CLOVER
              Alright.

She nods, used to this. And turning, Edward leaves...

137   INT. 1958, DEER ISLAND LODGE - EVENING   137

A HARP plays. People in their evening clothes talk and drink
as Edward comes in, crossing to Senator Russell. Mrs.
Russell, a stroke victim, sits in a wheelchair.

                    SENATOR RUSSELL
              Where's Clover?

                         EDWARD
              She's still getting dressed...

                    MRS. RUSSELL
              Clover?

                    SENATOR RUSSELL
              Yes dear, she'll be here soon...

Philip Allen comes over...

                    PHILIP ALLEN
              Good evening...

                         EDWARD
              Good evening...

Toddy turns to another couple. Edward and Philip find
themselves momentarily "alone." Philip quietly says:

                    PHILIP ALLEN
              The President's concerned about the
              growing popularity of a young neighbor
              of ours. I'd like you to be our "eyes
              and ears" down there. (then upbeat)
              Your son is becoming a real man, I
              hardly recognize him. Will he become
              one of us? His father's son?

                         EDWARD
              I hope he'll do whatever makes him
              happy.

                    PHILIP ALLEN
              That's the best any of us can hope for.
              Not everyone can be as lucky in life as
              we are to find our calling.

Philip paternally touches his shoulder...

                    PHILIP ALLEN (CONT'D)
              I have to get ready for my annual
              embarrassment.

He walks past his wife and the Russells...

                                              (CONTINUED)

137   CONTINUED:

                       TODDY ALLEN
        I was just telling Helen about our
        trip to Iran--what an elegant man the
        Shah is.

                       PHILIP ALLEN
        A great friend to America.

138   INT. 1958, EDWARD'S CABIN, DEER ISLAND - NIGHT   138

Clover at the dressing table, finishing dressing. Despite her
efforts, nothing seems to fit. A knock, and Edward Jr.,
almost 17, enters in a prep school jacket and hat.

                       EDWARD JR.
        There was an envelope for you at the
        desk, mother.

Clover crosses into a front room and takes the envelope.

                       CLOVER
        Thank you, darling.

                       EDWARD JR.
        You look lovely.

And he leaves. Clover opens the envelope, going back to the
dressing mirror. She takes out SURREPTITIOUS BLACK AND WHITE
PHOTOGRAPHS OF EDWARD AT THE BAR WITH LAURA, TALKING
INTIMATE. EDWARD AND LAURA IN THE STREET, KISSING HER CHEEK
WHILE IN A TAXI. GETTING INTO A TAXI TOGETHER. GOING WITH
LAURA INTO HER BUILDING. COMING OUT OF HER BUILDING ALONE.
Clover's motionless. She quietly takes another drink.

139   EXT. 1958, THE LODGE, DEER ISLAND - NIGHT   139

Clover, in evening gown, heels tip-tapping on the walk...

140   INT. 1958, THE LODGE, DINING ROOM, DEER ISLAND - NIGHT   140

People sit, drinking, laughing, watching Bonesmen dressed as
women singing and dancing to a piano, "There ain't nothin'
like a dame..." Clover enters, crossing the room to Edward. As
she reaches the table...

                       CLOVER
        You fucking son-of-a-bitch...! It's
        not enough for you to ignore me -- you
        have to humiliate me too...! You pig!
        You cheat on me! You cheat on our
        family! You pig.

As her father leads her out of the room, the piano starts to
play again, the men singing 'Ain't Nothing Like a Dam.'

A141   INT. 1958, EDWARD'S CABIN, DEER ISLAND - NIGHT   A141

Edward in the cabin, looking at the PHOTOS. Edward Jr. comes
out of the bedroom with his mother's luggage...He stops...

                       EDWARD JR.
        Mother forgot some of her things.

(CONTINUED)

>   EDWARD
>   Your mother's having a hard time right
>   now. She's been drinking too much.
>   She's going to get some help.

>   EDWARD JR.
>   I'd like to go with her to
>   grandfather's. I'd like to take her
>   there.

Edward is quiet...He nods 'okay.'

>   EDWARD JR. (CONT'D)
>   Mother says you don't care about her.
>   Is that true?

>   EDWARD
>   Of course I care about her. I love her
>   very much.

>   EDWARD JR.
>   See you back home.

141   EXT. 1958, DEER ISLAND, DOCK - NIGHT   141

A MOTOR LAUNCH idling. Edward Jr. and Clover, still in gown,
holding purse, stand on the deck of Launch. As it moves away,
wind blowing her hair, Clover, unsure of who she is anymore...

142   OMITTED   142

143   EXT. 1958, EDWARD'S CABIN PORCH, DEER ISLAND - NIGHT   143

Edward sits on porch chair, watching the Launch fade in the
distance. He looks out at water as music plays from Lodge...

144   EXT. 1958, THE LITTLE THEATRE, WASHINGTON - ANOTHER NIGHT 144

Laura and a few people wait. The lobby lights blink as people
rush to meet their dates, going inside. Laura knows her
"companion" isn't coming. A Man comes across the street:

>   RAY BROCCO
>   Are you Laura?

>   LAURA
>   Yes.

>   RAY BROCCO
>   I was asked to give you this.

He gives her a small box and walks off. She opens it. Inside is
her CROSS, Edward's "goodbye." As Laura moves down the street..

145   INT. 1961, COMMUNICATIONS CENTER, THE CIA - DAY   145

"Sunday, April 23 1961." EDWARD, followed by Brocco, comes
into the CIA Communications Center, filled with a few new
pieces of equipment from the past few years.

                                                        (CONTINUED)

145   CONTINUED: 145

                          COMMUNICATIONS OFFICER # 2
                    The call came in from Jo-Berg at 20:24
                    Zulu. It's one of Ulysses' Watch
                    Listed numbers.

A Woman's VOICE speaks Russian over the speakers...

                          EDWARD
                    Is Mr. Mironov here yet...

Ray gets on the phone. Getting his answer.

                          RAY BROCCO
                    He's in his office.

A145   INT 1961, VALENTIN'S OFFICE, THE CIA - DAY   A145

A Very small bare room. VALENTIN sits at his desk, smoking,
as Edward and Ray play a reel-to-reel of the WOMAN speaking
russian...

                          VALENTIN
                      (translating)
                    "...Not only in the soul of the
                    frightened yet happy and enraptured
                    Natasha, but in the whole house there
                    was a feeling of awe of something
                    important that was bound to happen..."
                    Don't you recognize that, Mother?
                    "Count Rostov took the girls to
                    Countess Bezukhova's..."

                          EDWARD
                    Tolstoy's, "War and Peace."

                          VALENTIN
                    Well of course. It's Stas's little
                    game. They're going through a normal
                    coding procedure... She's reading from
                    "War and Peace..." Whatever sequence
                    has been determined for the day
                    provides the indicator words... One
                    day it is every third word, and then
                    the code word. Another day it is every
                    fourth word. Another every second,
                    third and tenth word... Sometimes, it
                    is simply to fill the air to confuse
                    you...

As they listen...

                          EDWARD
                    What do you think?

                          VALENTIN
                    I think Stas has something to tell us.
                    She's repeated "babochka,"
                    "Butterfly," five times... It's her
                    identifier. Their code names always go
                    back at least one generation...
                          (MORE)

A145   CONTINUED: A145
                              VALENTIN (CONT'D)
                     For instance, "frog" would be in
                     actuality, "tadpole," or even,
                     "pond"... A "Butterfly" would then
                     be...

                              EDWARD
                     "Cocoon..."

Valentin nods, saying the word in Russian, "kokon."

                              EDWARD (CONT'D)
                     I don't remember hearing about anyone
                     by that name.

Edward gives Ray a signal to make a call. Ray picks up the
phone...

                              RAY BROCCO
                          (into phone)
                     Bracco. Division C. I want to check
                     the Bible for codename "Cocoon." And
                     if there's a 201, get it up here.

Edward looks around the room, always aware of his
surroundings. He notices the "Ulysses" book Arch Cummings
gave Valentin on a nearby bookshelf. A bookish, Older Woman
enters with a file, giving it to Ray...

                              OPERATIONS OFFICER # 2
                     Her name is Corrine Touré, aka "Miriam
                     Temesgen." She's a KGB swallow
                     stationed in Paris, January 1960...
                     She was last placed in
                     Cameroon...She's from Mali. She did
                     her schooling in Moscow... Our crypt
                     for her is "AF-Allegory."

Ray passes Edward the file. Inside is a surveillance photo of
a striking young BLACK WOMAN.

                              EDWARD
                     Are these the only photographs we
                     have?

                              OPERATIONS OFFICER # 2
                     Yes. They were taken on Soviet
                     National Day in Paris.

                              EDWARD
                     Reassign the files to us.

                              OPERATIONS OFFICER # 2
                     Yes, sir.

                              RAY BROCCO
                     Thank you.

A146   INT. 1961, EDWARD'S'S OFFICE, THE CIA - DAY   A146

Edward and Ray in the office, looking at "Miriam's" photo,
comparing it to the Woman in the PHOTO of the interracial
couple... There's more than a striking resemblance. As Edward
quietly looks at "Miriam's" photograph:

                                                        (CONTINUED)

A146   CONTINUED:

                        EDWARD
            It was too easy to identify her. I
            think they wanted us to...

                        EDWARD'S VOICE
            Would you like to learn how?

146   INT. 1958 EDWARD'S SUBURBAN HOUSE, STUDY - NIGHT   146

A TWEEZER GRASPS A THREAD. PULL BACK to see Edward at desk in
study making a ship for a bottle. Edward Jr. stands behind him,
watching. Edward gives his son the tweezer, passing the mantle.

                        EDWARD
            Gently...Don't force it. Careful...
            Watch the bow sprit... Careful....
            Perfect.

Edward Jr. carefully pulls the thread, pulling the masts
down. Very carefully he slips the ship into the bottle. They
both smile, proud. They look in each other's eyes until
Edward lowers his eyes, peering at the ship...

                        EDWARD JR.
            Our Glee Club has been chosen to
            compete in a national competition...
            Would you come with me, father?

Edward looks at him touched.

                        EDWARD
            Would you like me to?

                        EDWARD JR.
            I would very much.

The front door opens. There are footsteps on the stairs. It's
Clover. Whatever was left in her, has gone cold. She's home
again, willing to suffer, "A quiet life of desperation," for her
child.

                        CLOVER
            I'm sorry if I've hurt anyone.

                        EDWARD JR.
            I'll get your bags.

Clover and Edward look at each other. And as she walks to
their bedroom...

                        EDWARD
            It's very good to have you home.

And there's the sound of BOYS' VOICES singing, "Shenandoah."

147   OMITTED   147

148   INT. 1958, A PREPARATORY SCHOOL HALL - DAY   148

Prep School Glee Clubs, wait their turn to sing. With a
group, singing "Shenandoah," is Edward Jr.

                                                    (CONTINUED)

With the other parents, off by himself, sits Edward. His son
looks at him, grateful he's there, singing in lovely
harmony...   A shadow crosses over Edward and sits down...

                    A MAN'S VOICE
          Hello, mother...

It's Stas Siyanko, his TARTAR nearby, against a wall.

                    EDWARD
               (without turning)
          How was your trip?

                    STAS SIYANKO
          Smooth as silk... My F.B.I. escort
          made the trip here very pleasant...

Edward sees Sam Murach, smoking by a door. They exchange nods.

                    STAS SIYANKO (CONT'D)
          Which one is your son?

                    EDWARD
          Top row. Third from the right.

They listen to the Boys singing "Shenandoah."

                    STAS SIYANKO
          He's a handsome young man. Is he going
          to follow in his father's footsteps?

Edward is quiet...

                    EDWARD
          We're particularly concerned about
          Cuba. Your friend... He's too close to
          home.

                    STAS SIYANKO
          You don't appreciate him, how do you
          say it, "breathing down your neck?"

                    EDWARD
          If we go too far down that road, we
          will have a third world war...
          I don't think either of "us" wants a
          "real" war...

                    STAS SIYANKO
               (smiles, ironic)
          What would we do for a living then,
          Mother? (a beat) There can be no
          guarantees when it comes to
          revolutionaries...but I understand
          your position.

Even Edward manages a thin smile. They're quiet.

                    EDWARD
          If he keeps calling attention to
          himself, at some point, we may have to
          send him a surprise. I don't want it
          to come as a surprise to your people.

                                              (CONTINUED)

                         STAS SIYANKO
               He is very important to us. We would
               not like to be surprised... (beat) The
               situation in Berlin is becoming more
               difficult to manage. People are
               leaving East Germany every day... We
               might be forced to put a wall up
               between east and west Berlin. We will
               expect it to stay up.

                         EDWARD
               We won't climb the wall unless we have
               to... Don't make us have to.

                         STAS SIYANKO
               Then we see eye to eye.

                         EDWARD
               Eye to eye.

The Tartar comes over and asks something. Stas nods, and
Tartar leaves.

                         STAS SIYANKO
                    (a rare smile)
               It seems like he has to go to the
               bathroom every ten minutes... not a
               good recommendation for a bodyguard.

Edward smiles. And as they talk while the Boys are singing:

149   INT. 1958, MEN'S ROOM, PREPARATORY SCHOOL - DAY   149

The Tartar waits for one of two occupied stalls, another Man
behind him... One stall door opens, a robed Glee Club Member
coming out. Tartar motions to the Man behind him to take it:

                         THE TARTAR
               Please, please...

The Man nods a "thank you" and takes the available stall, the
Tartar still waiting. A flush, and Ray Bracco comes out of
the other stall, passing the Tartar. He washes his hands as
the Russian enters "Brocco's" stall, closing the door behind
him... And as Brocco leaves...

150   INT. 1958, THE PREPARATORY SCHOOL HALL - DAY   150

Edward and Stas sit with the parents, finishing their business.

                         STAS SIYANKO
               Give my regards to Valentin... I miss
               hearing him play the violin... Ask him
               to play the Second Movement of
               Tchaikovsky's Violin Concerto for
               you...He plays it so well... I have
               enjoyed working with your brother-in-
               law, John Russell... He's a sensitive
               man. Am I mistaken, Mother, or is
               there a sadness about him...? Do you
               think I can trust him? Or is he a
               plant, growing inside me...

                                              (CONTINUED)

150   CONTINUED: 150

        Edward doesn't say anything. Stas turns to go...

                        STAS SIYANKO (CONT'D)
                Premier Khrushchev is thinking of
                making a trip to your country. He
                wants to go to Disneyland when he
                comes. What ride would you recommend?

                        EDWARD
                I've never been to Disneyland, but I
                hear the Matterhorn is worth the ride.

                        STAS SIYANKO
                The Matterhorn, really? Thank you. Be
                well.

                        EDWARD
                Be well.

        Stas smiles, and leaves with his Tartar, following Murach's
        lead. Edward turns and sees his son looking up at him,
        shoulders hunched, unable to hide his deep hurt...

151   INT. 1960, EDWARD'S OFFICE, THE CIA - ANOTHER DAY   151

        JFK on TV, announcing his intention to run for President.
        Edward at desk, Valentin in a chair, watching. Ray comes in.

                        RAY BROCCO
                   (whispering to Edward)
                There's a KGB defection in progress in
                Stockholm...

152   INT. 1960, COMMUNICATIONS CENTER, THE CIA - DAY   152

        Edward and Ray in the Communications Center.

                        COMMUNICATIONS OFFICER # 3
                I'm receiving a signal, 5 x 5. We have
                a secure circuit with Stockholm.
                Station reports they have a Colonel
                Directorate K, Counterintelligence.

                        EDWARD
                Do we have a name...?

                        COMMUNICATIONS OFFICER # 3
                There's a two second delay.

153   INT. 1960, THE U.S. EMBASSY, STOCKHOLM - NIGHT   153

        A tall, good looking MAN enters an embassy with a Janitor
        mopping the floor, and a young half-asleep Duty Officer.

                        THE FIELD OFFICER
                May I help you, sir...?

                        VALENTIN # 2
                I need to speak to the CIA Station
                Chief.

        The Field Officer picks up the phone.

                                                          (CONTINUED)

153   CONTINUED: 153

                         THE FIELD OFFICER
               Mr. Granger has a visitor, Post # 1.

A moment, and a CIA Officer comes out and greets the Russian.

154   INT. 1960, COMMUNICATIONS CENTER, THE CIA - DAY   154

Over the speakers:

                         STATION CHIEF
               Passport, please.

155   INT. 1960, THE U.S. EMBASSY, STOCKHOLM - NIGHT   155

                         THE MAN
               I am a Colonel with the Committee of
               State Security...

                         STATION CHIEF
               What is your name?

                         THE MAN
               My name is Valentin Gregorievich
               Mironov...I am requesting asylum...

156   INT. 1960, NEW COMMUNICATIONS CENTER, THE CIA - DAY   156

Edward, hearing the all too familiar name, looks up.

157   INT. 1960, A HOTEL ROOM, WASHINGTON D.C. - DAY   157

An early familiar chain hotel. MEN stand and sit around a
HOTEL ROOM. Among them, Ray Brocco. In chair, naked, is the
"OTHER VALENTIN MIRONOV." PULL BACK and see Edward and
Valentin in an adjoining hotel room, looking through a TWO-
WAY MIRROR. Intelligence personnel monitor a tape recorder...

                         THE OTHER VALENTIN
               ...This other man, who says he is
               Valentin Mironov, is not who he
               pretends to be... His real name is
               Yuri Modin... he was Stas Siyanko's
               right hand... He is Stas's mole...

                         VALENTIN
               It is just Stas trying to discredit
               me, Mother...

Edward is quiet. As he studies the "Other," naked Valentin.

158   INT. 1960, THE HOTEL ROOM, WASHINGTON D.C. - DAY   158

Ray Brocco gets in the man's face, rough...

                         RAY BROCCO
               What is your name?

                         THE OTHER VALENTIN
               My name is Valentin Gregorievich
               Miranov.
                         (MORE)

                                               (CONTINUED)

158   CONTINUED: 158

                            THE OTHER VALENTIN (CONT'D)
                    I was born in Bobrujsk in 1924. I
                    attended the State Institute of
                    International Relations, served for
                    three years in Naval Intelligence... My
                    wife's name is Tamara Markovskaya. My
                    children's names are Anatoliy and
                    Sergei... My father is a cellist... I
                    play violin... All I want is freedom...

        Ray slaps him, knocking him and the chair over. Two
        Operations Officers pick him up, putting him back in chair.

                            RAY BROCCO
                    What's your name?

        Same answer. He's slapped again... The routine continues,
        same questions, same answers... slap, slap, slap...

159   INT. 1960, THE ADJOINING HOTEL ROOM - LATE AFTERNOON   159

        The man, naked, a hood over his head. The windows are wide
        open, the room freezing cold. His interrogators wear coats.

                            RAY BROCCO
                    What is your name?

                            THE OTHER VALENTIN
                            (crying, exhausted)
                    My name is Valentin Gregorievich
                    Mironov... I was born in Bobrujsk... I
                    am freezing...

160   INT. 1960, THE ADJOINING HOTEL ROOM - LATE AFTERNOON   160

        Edward looks at a TAB of medicine with "Sandoz" written on it.

                            TECHNICAL SERVICES OFFICER
                    It's lysergic acid diethylamide,
                    called LSD... There has been some very
                    favorable results as a truth serum.

        Edward gives the tab back to the man... And nods to try it...

161   INT. 1960, THE HOTEL ROOM - NIGHT   161

        The OTHER VALENTIN, hood off now, face bloodied, is still
        naked in a chair. He has a look of drugged confusion.

                            RAY BROCCO
                    What is your name?

                            THE OTHER VALENTIN
                    My name is Valentin Gregorievich
                    Mironov....
                            (starts to cry, rambling)
                    My children's names are Anatoliy and
                    Sergei... sweet little Anatoliy, he
                    sings like a bird...

        He sings a children's song in Russian...

(CONTINUED)

> THE OTHER VALENTIN (CONT'D)
> When I was a boy I remember taking a
> train to Moscow with my father...
>   (as if on train, reciting)
> ...Bobrujsk, Kricov, Roslavl,
> Malojaroslavec, Odincove...

He gets to his feet.

> THE OTHER VALENTIN (CONT'D)
> ...We saw the May Day parade... Stalin
> rode in an open car... (points) Look
> papa it's him...

Like a little Boy he salutes their leader, SINGING the
Russian National Anthem of that time, "The Internationale..."
Suddenly he's quiet, on some LSD plane.

> THE OTHER VALENTIN (CONT'D)
> Every piece of intelligence
> information that you get is created by
> the KGB... When the Agency has a cold
> the KGB sneezes...
>   (whispering, a secret)
> Soviet power is a myth. A great show.
> There are no spare parts... nothing
> works... It is nothing but painted
> rust...
>   (walking around)
> You need to keep the Russian myth
> alive to maintain your military
> industrial complex... Your system
> depends on Russia being perceived as a
> mortal threat... It isn't a threat, it
> was never a threat, it will never be a
> threat... It is a bloated rotted cow.

He's quiet again... And suddenly, he shouts...

> THE OTHER VALENTIN (CONT'D)
> I am Valentin Gregorievich Mironov...!
> And I am free...!

He runs to a window and dives through... falling to the street.

162   INT.   1960, THE ADJOINING HOTEL ROOM - NIGHT   162

Edward is still. He turns to look at the "real" Valentin...

> VALENTIN
> If you would like, I'll be glad to take
> the "truth" serum, Edward. I have
> nothing to hide... I am who I say I am.

Edward quietly looks at him. He shakes "no."

> EDWARD
>   (dark, cold)
> I trust you.

And he leaves, his shoulders hunched, head down...

163   EXT. 1960, THE YALE CATHEDRAL, QUADRANGLE - DAY   163

Families gather with their graduates. Edward Jr., nearly 21,
in cap and gown, stands with his family. Clover affectionately
holds his arm. Grown extremely heavy, it's as if she's grown a
second skin, her last line of defense... Edward has become the
long shadow, starting to sink into himself, his clothes
seeming to bunch in on him. A thin, bespectacled BLACK MAN, a
graduate, distinctly African, comes over to them.

                    EDWARD JR.
          Mother and Father, this is my good
          friend Thomas Lumumba. Mr. Lumumba's
          uncle will soon be the first President
          of the Congo...

                    THOMAS LUMUMBA
          It is a very great honor... Would it
          be possible to take your picture...?

Without warning he takes their picture with a Polaroid.
Edward, protectively, looks away... "CLICK." The Polaroid
comes to life... Edward, a blur, Edward Jr. proud of himself,
and the corpulent Clover, the Edward Wilson family...

164   INT. 1960, SKULL AND BONES MEETING ROOM, YALE - NIGHT   164

A "1939" PHOTO of Skull and Bones. PULL BACK to Edward looking
at photo, in meeting room with cases of mementoes, class photos,
and history of Skull and Bones. The Bonesmen, with their
fathers, stand together. Edward turns to stand by Edward Jr. A
Young Man, the world in the palm of his hand, addresses them:

                    THE YOUNG MAN
          We send those who are leaving us to go
          into the world, with the knowledge,
          wherever they go, whatever they do,
          they will never be alone, they will
          always be one of us... And we say...
          Bonesmen...!

                    THE BONESMEN
               (as one)
          All here!

                    EDWARD
               (a beat late)
          All here.

165   INT. 1960, SKULL AND BONES BASEMENT CORRIDOR - LATER   165

Edward and Edward Jr. walk the dimly lit corridor. They pass the
room where their most intimate secrets were shared. Drawn to it,
they go into room, with all its memories, and stand quietly.

                    EDWARD JR.
          What did you tell them? What was your
          secret?

                    EDWARD
          I told them about your grandfather.

                         EDWARD JR.
               You never talk about it.

               He was a lonely, troubled man. I wish
               I had got to know him (he looks at his
               son) That won't happen to us. (after a
               beat, remembering) The last thing he
               said to me was to never do anything
               I'd be ashamed of...

                         EDWARD JR. (CONT'D)
               Have you, father?

                         EDWARD
               I've tried not to.

They're quiet. Each with their own thoughts...Edward Jr.
Lights a cigarette.

                         EDWARD (CONT'D)
               I didn't know you smoked.

                         EDWARD JR.
               There are a few things you don't know
               me...I've spoken to a recruiter here..
               I would like very much to join CIA...

Edward is dead still, taken off guard, anguished by the
thought. He can't hide his feelings.

                         EDWARD
               There are a lot of things you can do.
               I want you to think about it
               carefully.

                         EDWARD JR.
               I have thought about it. It's what I
               want. I want to join the Agency. I
               want you to be proud.

                         EDWARD
               I am proud.

                         EDWARD JR.
               I've made up my mind, father.

Edward is quiet, his heart breaking. Before he can say
anything, the other fathers and sons, holding candles, come
along, singing the "Whiffenpoof Song." Edward looks at his
son, eyes aglow, filled with inspiration...

A166   INT. 1960, EDWARD'S BEDROOM, VIRGINIA - NIGHT   A166

Clover, in her bathrobe, getting ready for bed...Edward,
still dressed from work, sits on the bed...

                         CLOVER
               You could do something to stop him!

                         EDWARD
               He's a grown man. It's his life.

                                              (CONTINUED)

                              CLOVER
                    He's still a boy. He doesn't know what
                    he's getting into. You could stop him.

                              EDWARD
                    I thought of that. But I can't tell
                    him what to do.

                              CLOVER
                    Yes, you can.

                              EDWARD
                    No I can't.

                              CLOVER
                    Yes, you can...! He's doing it for
                    you. He thinks you'll be proud of him.
                    He thinks it'll make him closer to
                    you... You could have them reject
                    him....

Edward doesn't answer.

                              CLOVER (CONT'D)
                    Why would I expect you to help him.
                    You've never done anything for anybody
                    but yourself.

                              EDWARD
                    That's unfair.

                              CLOVER
                    You abandon people when they need you
                    the-

                              EDWARD
                    That's unfair. I don't abandon people.

Their argument grows, it's messy, they overlap each other...

                              CLOVER
                    Yes, you do. You abandon people.

                              EDWARD
                    I've stood by you for twenty-two
                    years!

                              CLOVER
                    Stood by me! You don't know what it
                    means to stand by somebody.

                              EDWARD
                    I've stood by him.

                              CLOVER
                    You ignored him!

                              EDWARD
                    I stood by him. I married you because
                    of him!

It's quiet.

                                                        (CONTINUED)

                          CLOVER
            I know you don't love me. But you love
            him, and no matter what it takes, you
            should protect him. You're his father.

                          EDWARD
            I don't need you to tell me I have to
            protect my own son.

                          CLOVER
            Please Edward, just promise me that
            you will.

                          EDWARD
            I promise.
                (a beat)
            I know how to protect my son.

166   INT. 1960, EDWARD'S OFFICE, THE CIA - EARLY MORNING   166

       Edward, at desk, peers at a PHOTOGRAPH on the front page of a
       NEWSPAPER of Castro. Among the people behind him, just
       recognizable, is Stas Siyanko... Edward looks up at Ray...

                          EDWARD
            I want to see a man about a hat.

167   EXT. 1960, FAR ROCKAWAY, NEW YORK - DAY   167

       Small but comfortable houses near the beach. Old people sit
       on chairs on front lawns as children come and go from the
       beach. Waiting in a car is Sam Murach. Standing inside a
       screened-in front porch, waiting, is Edward. A large man
       opens the front door.

                          EDWARD
            Mr. Carlson for Mr. Palmi.

                          PALMI'S GUARD
            Wait here.

168   INT. 1960, THE HOUSE IN FAR ROCKAWAY, NEW YORK - DAY   168

       The large man returns...

                          PALMI'S GUARD
            Mr. Carlson, Mr. Palmi asks that you
            please come in...

       Edward follows the Man into the foyer kitchen. Dressed
       casually, is a dark, somber man, in his 50's... JOSEPH PALMI.

                          PALMI'S GUARD (CONT'D)
            Joe...Mr. Carlson.

                          JOSEPH PALMI
            Sit down. Tina, the kids. Do you want
            coffee? Water? Something?

       Edward doesn't. A Young Woman with two small children in
       their bathing suits comes in.

                                                    (CONTINUED)

                              PALMI'S DAUGHTER
                    Come on, kids.

                              EDWARD
                    Is there someplace else we can go?

The message is understood.

                              JOSEPH PALMI
                    Let's go outside.

169   EXT. PALMI'S PATIO, FAR ROCKAWAY - DAY   169

Palmi and Edward walk outside to the patio and sit down...
His daughter and kids follow...

                              PALMI'S DAUGHTER
                    Daddy, we're going to the beach... You
                    going to come down at all...?

                              JOSEPH PALMI
                    I'll be there soon... Make sure they
                    don't go in the water without somebody
                    watching them...

                              PALMI'S DAUGHTER
                    No. I'm going to let them drown...
                    Let's go kids...

                              JOSEPH PALMI
                    Where's their shoes...? They're going
                    to burn their feet...

                              PALMI'S DAUGHTER
                    We're getting their shoes...

And they go out...

                              JOSEPH PALMI
                    So what about you? You have any
                    children?

                              EDWARD
                    No, I'm afraid I don't...

The large man sets down some coffee...

                              PALMI'S GUARD
                    Coffee, Joe.

                              JOSEPH PALMI
                    You sure you don't want any coffee?

                              EDWARD
                    No thank you.

                              JOSEPH PALMI
                    So what do you want to talk about?

(CONTINUED)

                              EDWARD
                    The government is about to deport you
                    for certain activities.

                              JOSEPH PALMI
                    I've lived here since I was forty days
                    old...What does that make me, an
                    Italian? I'm an American...and these
                    scumbags are trying to send me back...

                              EDWARD
                    I could have the deportation order
                    "reviewed..." have you classified as
                    "highly sensitive" for national
                    security. I could take the Government
                    off your back

                              JOSEPH PALMI
                    You's the guys that scare me... It's
                    people like you that make big wars...

                              EDWARD
                    No, we make sure the wars are small
                    ones, Mr. Palmi...

                              JOSEPH PALMI
                    Let me ask you something... We
                    [Italians] have our families, our
                    church... The Irish, they have their
                    homeland.. The Jews, they got
                    traditions... Even the niggers have
                    music... Tell me something, Mr.
                    Carlson, what do you people have...?

                              EDWARD
                    The United States of America... the
                    rest of you are just visiting...

          They look at each other, a mutual contempt... After a moment:

                              JOSEPH PALMI
                    What do you want with me?

170   EXT. 1960, HAVANA, CUBA - ANOTHER DAY   170

          And we see the Caribbean Island so close to home.

171   INT. 1960, THE PRESIDENT'S OFFICE, HAVANA, CUBA - DAY   171

          A cigar is taken out of a box. Castro is on the phone, talking.
          His other phone rings and he listens...He takes the cigar out
          of his mouth.

                              EL PRESIDENTE
                         (listens, nodding)
                    Si... Si... gracias...

          He hangs up. He presses an intercom, asking for somebody. A
          uniformed AIDE comes in. Presidente offers him the "cigar."
          The man shakes "no, gracias."

                                                      (CONTINUED)

171   CONTINUED: 171

                         EL PRESIDENTE (CONT'D)
            Come on, smoke a cigar.

                         THE AIDE
            No thank you. I don't smoke in the
            morning.

                         EL PRESIDENTE
            Sure?

                         THE AIDE
            Sure.

Castro says something to his Officers, and they take the man
out onto a courtyard below. Castro looks out the window at
the courtyard. The phone rings. He takes up phone and we hear
him talking to a child in Spanish (subtitled).

                         EL PRESIDENTE
            Hello, sweetheart. How was school today?
            What did you learn?

As he talks, he watches the Aide, terrified, soldiers at a
distance, their weapons trained on him. The man lights the
"cigar," made to smoke it. An ash forms, slowly getting
longer and longer with each puff. Tears run down his face...
A loud explosion... and El Commandante lights a cigar...

172   INT. 1960, A WASHINGTON HOTEL ROOM - NIGHT   172

Edward, Hayes, a Latin Man, GEN. HECTOR SUAREZ and four Other
Officers we've seen before, sit around a hotel room, the
Capitol Building visible out the window.

                         RICHARD HAYES
            ...The President, if asked, will of
            course deny any knowledge... but we've
            been given his blessings to move
            ahead... I will coordinate security
            and personnel. Mr. Robbins has made
            arrangements with our friends on Wall
            Street for "off the books" financing.
            Mr. Ellis will coordinate supplies.
            General Suarez will coordinate
            logistics. Mr. Wilson, who conceived
            of this action, will run the show.

He looks over at Edward to say something...

                         EDWARD
            We're designating this "Operation
            Zapata"...Back channel, "Manifest
            Destiny. This has the highest level of
            denialbility, because the operation
            does not exist.

173   EXT. 1961, EDWARD'S PORCH, DEER ISLAND - DAY   173

Edward and Edward Jr. sit outside their cabin...

173   CONTINUED:

                              EDWARD JR.
                    I don't know how you felt after your
                    first assignment... But I feel such a
                    great love for my country...

                              EDWARD
                         (impassive)
                    I'm glad you feel that way...

                              EDWARD JR.
                    My station chief has extended my tour
                    in the Congo.

                              EDWARD
                    Yes, I heard...

Edward is quiet, watching the water lap against the shore.

                              EDWARD (CONT'D)
                    Never trust a soul, Edward. Not a soul.

Edward Jr., innocent, sees how deadly serious he is...

                              EDWARD JR.
                    Do you trust me, father?

                              EDWARD
                    I don't think you would ever
                    disappoint me.

                              EDWARD JR.
                    What does that mean?

                              EDWARD
                    It means I love you and don't want
                    anything to happen to you.

And that's as big as it gets...

                              EDWARD (CONT'D)
                    Before you go out in the field on an
                    assignment, I want you to always check
                    with me first...

Edward Jr. nods... As they walk off...

174   EXT. 1961, EDWARD'S CABIN, DEER ISLAND - EARLY EVENING   174

Edward Jr. taking a bath. He overhears something outside the
window.

                              PHILIP ALLEN
                    Rocking Chair wants the "noise level"
                    of the operation turned down. How many
                    men will be involved?

                              EDWARD
                    1500.

                              PHILIP ALLEN
                    How many aren't Cuban exiles? How many
                    Americans?

(CONTINUED)

                         EDWARD
            Two.

                         PHILIP ALLEN
            That's good...

                         EDWARD'S VOICE
            And we're scrapping Trinidad City as
            our primary landing site...

Edward Jr. gets out of the tub, wrapping a towel around
himself. He looks out the screened bathroom window...He sees
Edward with Philip Allen and Richard Hayes on a porch along
the side of the house...quietly talking...The sound of water
dripping into the tub causes Edward to turn. He can't see
inside, but senses someone. Edward Jr., feeling like he
shouldn't hear this, starts to close the window. But he can't
help himself... listening...

                         EDWARD
            ...Tell him we're going instead to
            "Bahia de Cochinos," "The Bay of Pigs.
            It's a remote beach. The noise level
            will be way down.

                         PHILIP ALLEN
            That's good. See you soon...

After Edward finishes with Allen and Hayes, Edward Jr.
crosses to his bedroom... Edward comes inside to Edward Jr.'s
Room. He knocks. He opens the door and sees Edward Jr. in
his underwear, knowing he's heard certain things...

                         EDWARD
            Did you hear what we were saying?

                         EDWARD JR.
            I didn't hear anything.

                         EDWARD
            Well if something was heard, it
            shouldn't leave this room.

                         EDWARD JR.
            I know that father. We do work for the
            same people.

Edward is quiet, seeing what he's done to him. The door opens
and a maid comes in.

                         EDWARD
            Please knock, before you enter.

                         MAID
            Sorry, sir.

                         EDWARD JR.
            It's alright, father.

Edward looks at his son...

                                                          (CONTINUED)

174   CONTINUED: (2)

                         EDWARD
                Shut the window.

And Edward leaves...

175   INT. 1961, THE LODGE, DINING ROOM, DEER ISLAND - NIGHT   175

The alumni and their families sit at their tables. Only
Edward's family is left at his table. Where Senator Russell
and John once sat, are place names and plates turned over
with a piece of black ribbon on them. Edward looks around.
Philip and Toddy now sit with Hayes. Philip and Edward
exchange nods. An Old Man POUNDS his cane twice on the floor.
The Bonesmen come to their feet and say as one:

                         BONESMEN MC
                Bonesmen... All here!

They give a rousing SHOUT and take their seats again...

                         BONESMEN MC (CONT'D)
                Reverend Christiansen will offer
                grace...

                         CLOVER
                "The Agency" first, God second...

Edward and Clover look at each other as the Reverend leads the
room in prayer.

                         REVEREND CHRISTIANSON
                Thank you for bringing us safely here
                to be with our brothers and loved ones
                again...Our prayers are with our
                brothers whom God has seen fit to take
                into his gentle arms this year...Mr.
                Stephen Loomis Evans...Mr. Laughlin
                Morris B. Taylor...and the
                Honorable Senator James Adams Russell.

And as the Reverend continues the prayer, "Dear Lord we ask
for your guidance, and your forbearance..."

176   INT. 1961, THE LODGE - NIGHT, LATER   176

Lights lowered, people drink and talk at their tables. Others
dance as A BIG BAND plays "I'm gonna love you, like nobody's
loved you..." Edward Jr. dances with a smiling debutante
while Edward and Clover sit, watching the dancers. All the
wasted years seem to wash over them like saltwater...

                         EDWARD
                Would you like to dance, Clover?

                         CLOVER
                I haven't been Clover in a long time.

                         EDWARD
                I know.

                                                    (CONTINUED)

176   CONTINUED: 176

He offers his hand. She hesitates, then takes his hand, as he
takes her to dance. They quietly move around the dance floor.
She looks at him. He's quiet. After some moments:

                    CLOVER
          I'm going to Phoenix, to live with my
          mother.

Edward is quiet...And as they dance, trying to remember who they
were, Edward Jr. looks over at them. Needing someone to hold, he
holds his partner close.

177   INT. 1961, EDWARD'S OFFICE, THE CIA - MORNING - APRIL 23 177

                    THE WOMAN'S VOICE (OVER)
          "You are safe here with me..."

Edward, at desk, tape-recorder turning, photo of inter-racial
couple and BLOW-UPS on desk. Brocco and two Men are present.

                    TECHNICAL OFFICER # 2
          Based on the ringing of the church
          bell, we're going on the assumption
          that the recording was made at the
          same time as the photo was taken.
          We've checked the schedules for
          flights leaving major airports on or
          around 10:00 at night for a two week
          period... There were flights leaving
          nine cities... Of those nine, seven
          were places that have significant
          contacts with the Russians to have
          Russian automobiles there... Six were
          places that also would potentially
          have a fan made in Belgium. Five of
          those places were also either tropical
          or in their summer season... Three of
          those were places where French is
          spoken... We think the tape was made
          in either Dakar, Abidjan, or Congo-
          Leo.

Edward looks up, hearing the one country he so desperately
didn't want to hear, but already knew in his heart.

                    EDWARD
          The Congo.

                    TECHNICAL OFFICER # 2
          Yes that's what we believe sir.

                    EDWARD
          Thank you.

And the men leave Edward alone, with his thoughts...

178   EXT. 1961, LEOPOLDVILLE, THE CONGO - DAY   178

Posters of Lumumba cover buildings. Edward, in raincoat,
walks through the crowded streets. A CHURCH BELL RINGS. He
turns the corner and sees a very OLD BELGIAN CHURCH, its bell
ringing. He comes around a corner and slows.

                                                      (CONTINUED)

178   CONTINUED:

In an apartment's window, blowing from a breeze, are the
curtains with the baobab pattern on them. He enters building.

179   INT. 1961, LEOPOLDVILLE APARTMENT BUILDING, CONGO - DAY   179

He comes along a hallway to the end apartment. He knocks.
It's quiet. He tries it, the knob turns. He steps inside...

180   INT. 1961, LEOPOLDVILLE APARTMENT, THE CONGO - DAY   180

It's dark. Edward goes into the bedroom. On a chair, is Stas.

                    STAS SIYANKO
              Hello, Mother.

Edward takes in the room. The nightstand with the clock, the
standing fan... The electrical outlet...And on the dresser by
a lamp, what was so difficult in the photograph to see, the
SHIP IN THE BOTTLE Edward made with his son.

                    STAS SIYANKO (CONT'D)
                 (meaning the situation)
              I'm sorry about this...(beat) Can I
              play something for you, Mother?

Edward motions at the wall outlet.

                    STAS SIYANKO (CONT'D)
              It is all gone... the tape recorders,
              the cameras... there is nothing else
              to know...

Edward is still.

                    STAS SIYANKO (CONT'D)
              Would you like to see for yourself?

Stas goes out and opens the door to the adjacent apartment,
revealing an empty apartment. Edward looks around...

                    STAS SIYANKO (CONT'D)
              You have to trust me, Mother. I may be
              the only one left you can trust.

Edward nods, trusting him... Stas turns on a reel-to-reel
TAPE RECORDER: we hear INTIMATE BREATHING... Then:

                    THE WOMAN'S VOICE (V.O.)
              "You are safe here with me..."

...and we hear Edward Jr.'s VOICE, intimate, whispering...

                    EDWARD JR. (V.O.)
                 (guilt ridden)
              "...He was standing out in back,
              talking...I had heard something I
              wasn't supposed to...He knew I had
              listened to his conversation..."
                 (after a beat, his deepest fears) I'm
              afraid of him. Everything's a
              secret...(and most of all) I
              disappointed him.

                                               (CONTINUED)

                    THE YOUNG WOMAN (V.O.)
          "You didn't do anything wrong. You
          were brought up on secrets. What did
          he expect...?" (and out of the quiet)
          "What was such a big secret, that his
          own son couldn't know?"

                    EDWARD JR. (V.O.)
                  (preoccupied, not
                   thinking)
          "...I heard him say they're going to
          invade Cuba...at a place called 'The
          Bay of Pigs'"

                    THE YOUNG WOMAN (V.O.)
                  (whispers, lovingly)
          "It's alright, darling... You haven't
          done anything wrong... You can tell me
          anything..." "I love you..." People who
          really love each other don't have
          secrets...I have something to tell
          you."

She whispers something intimate to him, inaudible. He
whispers back, "I love you so much..." The tape ends. Edward
is still.

                    STAS SIYANKO
          Her name is Corrine Temesgen, She's
          been an active asset of ours for some
          time...Until now. We can protect
          him... make him safe... Nobody would
          know...Not even him...They will be
          together... She loves him. Sometimes
          even spies fall in love...

Edward doesn't say anything.

                    STAS SIYANKO (CONT'D)
          All it would require, was for you, to
          sit in place...and help us, when your
          help is needed...

Edward is quiet.

                    STAS SIYANKO (CONT'D)
          I thought you'd like to see this.

Stas takes out a photo of Edward Jr.'s girlfriend from his
pocket and hands it to Edward.

                    STAS SIYANKO (CONT'D)
          She's a very pretty girl, it's easy to
          see why he fell for her.

Stas sits on the bed and takes the picture back.

                    STAS SIYANKO (CONT'D)
          I know it's an extremely difficult
          situation for you. But I'm afraid I'm
          going to need your answer very soon.
                  (MORE)

(CONTINUED)

180   CONTINUED: (2)   180

                        STAS SIYANKO (CONT'D)
                  Now you have to decide, what is of
                  more importance to you, your country
                  or your son?

They look each other in the eye, and Stas turns and leaves.
The door closes... Edward, immersed in the silence... He looks
at the ship in the bottle. He takes it in his hand...peering
at it. He hears a door open, Edward Jr. coming in...

                        EDWARD JR.
                  Father...? What are you doing here?

Edward, despite Stas's assurances, takes him into hallway.

181   INT. 1961, LEOPOLDVILLE, APARTMENT ROOF - DAY   181

                        EDWARD
                  ...She's not a friendly, Edward...

                        EDWARD JR.
                  I don't believe you...

                        EDWARD
                  She's a Russian agent... her real name
                  is --

                        EDWARD JR.
                        (shakes, "no," angrily)
                  Why should I believe you? You told me
                  yourself, not to trust anybody... You're
                  the master at creating the truth.
                        (steadfast)
                  I don't care what you say. I love her...
                  I asked her to marry me. I won't let you
                  take that away from me...

                        EDWARD
                  I can't protect you, Edward... I can't
                  keep you safe anymore...

                        EDWARD JR.
                  Safe? I never felt safe, father... I
                  was always frightened. I lived in fear
                  something awful was always going to
                  happen to you, to mother, to me...I
                  was always afraid. Why was it so hard
                  for you to love us, to love mother, to
                  love me.

He looks at Edward with disdain. Edward suddenly embraces him.
Edward Jr. pushes him away and goes down stairs. Edward looks
out over the square, seeing his son move off, left standing
alone, his coat seeming to hide him like a secret...

A182 EXT. 1961, CIA WASHINGTON D.C. - NIGHT   A182

Philip Allen exits building, his car waiting for him. His
driver helps him in. On the seat is a box of swiss chocolates.

                        PHILIP ALLEN
                  Where did these come from?

                                                        (CONTINUED)

A182   CONTINUED:

                         HIS DRIVER
               They were in the car. I thought you
               had them sent down.

          Philip opens the box. Under the chocolates are papers. Copies
          of swiss bank statements. As he quietly closes the box...

                         PHILIP ALLEN
               Home.

182   EXT. 1961, LANGLEY, MCLEAN, VIRGINIA - DAY   182

          "TUESDAY, APRIL 25, 1961." A Taxi pulls up. Edward gets out,
          briefcase in hand, on the edge of some woods in front of a
          massive BUILDING under construction, near completion,
          Security Fence around perimeter, a sign on the fence, "Bureau
          of Public Roads." He goes along walkway toward building. Up
          the steps, he stops at the threshold. He sees carved into the
          stone above the doorway, "The Truth Shall Make You Free."

183   INT. 1961, THE NEW CIA BUILDING, MCLEAN, VIRGINIA - DAY 183

          A large empty rotunda

                         RICHARD HAYES' VOICE
               Mr. Wilson.

          Edward turns to see Richard Hayes...

                         EDWARD
               Mr. Hayes.

                         RICHARD HAYES
               Have you been here before, Mother?

                         EDWARD
               I haven't had the time.

          They both look at the quote on the wall.

                         EDWARD (CONT'D)
               Who's idea was that?

                         RICHARD HAYES
               It's classified.

          As they walk away from the lobby and into a long corridor...

                         RICHARD HAYES (CONT'D)
               Mr. Allen has notified the President
               he will resign. Something about swiss
               bank accounts. It seems the greedy
               bastard has been hiding money away for
               years. Hasn't paid a dollar's taxes.
               Do you want to laugh? Whoever had the
               statements, sent them to him in a box
               of swiss chocolates... It wasn't you,
               was it, Mother?

          He laughs. Edward doesn't.

                                                          (CONTINUED)

> RICHARD HAYES (CONT'D)
> The President has asked me to become
> Director of CIA and do a complete
> "housecleaning" at my discretion. I
> need someone I can trust...After all,
> we are still brothers...

> EDWARD
> Why wouldn't you fire me, Mr Hayes?
> The Bay of Pigs was on my watch. It
> was my operation. Why keep me?

> RICHARD HAYES
> This building doesn't get built
> without you. You are CIA's heart and
> soul. (a beat) And who knows, maybe
> you have some secret in that safe of
> yours about me...

He smiles, eternally boyish, and turns, walking down hallway.

> RICHARD HAYES (CONT'D)
> I understand your son has fallen in
> love. He's planning to get married...
> Do you think that's a wise idea? He's
> very young, and from what I hear,
> impressionable. I hope it doesn't
> effect his judgment. That would become
> a problem. A problem for all of us. I
> hope he has the heart for this work...
> You know as well as anyone you have to
> distance yourself from your feelings.
> Love, in our world, can be a dangerous
> weapon... In some ways I'm glad I
> never had children. They can break
> your heart.

And still Edward doesn't say anything...After some moments.

> RICHARD HAYES (CONT'D)
> Let's put this Bay Of Pigs behind us.
> The president is concerned about
> Southeast Asia...We can take the
> gloves off. We won't have to be
> gentleman anymore...(motioning)
> This whole wing will be your part of
> the "world," counterintelligence...

They move down a corridor by unfinished rooms without doors.
Edward looks in: one with wires coming out of wall; another,
a light fixture dangling from the ceiling; another,
television monitors stacked on top of each other; another, a
conference table and no chairs. Hayes slows by some gaping
holes in wall.

> RICHARD HAYES (CONT'D)
> There are specifications for seven
> permanent safes... For the
> "gatekeeper" of the kingdom...Go take
> a look around.

Edward is quiet...

                                                  (CONTINUED)

183   CONTINUED: (2)   183

                         RICHARD HAYES (CONT'D)
                I have an oversight meeting... Can you
                imagine, Mother... they think they can
                look in our closet...(his smile) Like
                we'll let them. (he slows) I remember
                a senator once asked me, when we talk
                about CIA, why we don't ever use the
                word "the" in front of it... I ask
                him, do you put "the" in front of God?

Hayes smiles at the thought. Edward doesn't. That said,
Richard turns, going out a stairway door and disappearing,
the door closing behind him. Motionless, peering out his
glasses, Edward stands in the empty hallway...CIA's heart and
soul...

184   Omitted   184

A185   INT. OLD CIA HALLWAY - LATE NIGHT   A185

We see Edward, coming out of his office, putting on his hat,
buttoning his coat, moving off along the familiar hallway.
Something crosses his mind. He slows at an office door. He
tries the door. It's locked.

B185   INT. OLD CIA OFFICE HALLWAY - NIGHT SHORTLY LATER   B185

We see Edward being let into the office by a bulky,
plainclothes, security guard. The man leaves.

185   INT. VALETIN'S OFFICE - LATE NIGHT   185

We see Edward has come into Valentin's office. He stands,
hands in pockets, looking at the office. The objects we had
previously seen him observe, the photo of Valentin and his
family, the desk calender, a file folder, etc. He goes over
to the photograph, takes it up, and suddenly takes the
photograph out of the frame, looking at the back of it.
There's nothing unusual there. He replaces it. He stops for a
moment to look at the office again and he remembers, looking
at the Ulysses book on the shelf. And there's a momentary
memory of Arch giving the book to Valentin, and Valentin's
emotional response. He sees the book has a slip of paper, "a
trap" as a bookmark? He opens the book. He leafs through the
pages. There doesn't seem to be anything unusual about it. He
delicately feels the inside of the front cover, feeling for
something. And all of a sudden he tears open the inside front
cover to discover a hidden passport, money, and an escape
plan. As he stands motionless, the book in his hand...

A186   EXT. 1961, HALLWAY, VALENTIN'S APARTMENT - LATE AT NIGHT A186

Edward, standing in an empty hallway, briefcase in hand,
knocks on a door. Valentin, in underwear, awakened from a
drunk sleep, opens door.

                         VALENTIN
                Is there something wrong?

                         EDWARD
                I was on my way home and I had this
                need to hear you play the violin.

                                                          (CONTINUED)

> VALENTIN
> Play? The violin?

> EDWARD
> May I sit down?

> VALENTIN
> Of course. Would you like a drink?

> EDWARD
> No thank you...I heard it distinctly.
> I couldn't get it out of my head.
> Tchaikovsky's Violin Concerto. The
> Second Movement. Stas's favorite.

> VALENTIN
> Yes, he loves that piece. (arrogantly)
> He says the way I play it, it breaks
> your heart. Please, I am so tired.
> Can't it wait until tomorrow.

> EDWARD
> (adamant, shakes 'no')
> Who knows what tomorrow will bring? I
> would appreciate it. If you could play
> it.

> VALENTIN
> Now?

> EDWARD
> Now.

> VALENTIN
> If it is that important to you.

Valentin gets his violin, shaking off the residue of a
drunken sleep, still in his underwear. He plays the
Tchaikovsky for Edward, particularly heart rending. While he
plays...

> EDWARD
> That's enough. I just wanted to hear
> something from you that was true.

Edward takes out the Ulysses book and hands it to Valentin.
He gets up, and walks out the door. A moment and TWO YOUNG
FBI MEN enter.

> FBI MAN
> FBI. Get up. Leave that alone. Turn
> around. Let's go.

And they begin to cuff him...

C186   EXT. VALENTIN'S APARTMENT, WASHINGTON D.C. - NIGHT   C186

Edward stands outside with Sam Murach...

> EDWARD
> Have you located Arch Cummings yet?

C186   CONTINUED: C186

                         SAM MURACH
                 Not yet.

Edward nods as Valentin is brought out and put into a car...

                         VALENTIN
                 Where are you taking me. I can't go
                 home. You know won't trust me anymore.
                 You know what they'll do to me.
                 Edward. Edward! You can still save me.
                 Edward!

Edward is quiet. Edward and Murach exchange a final look, and
Edward walks off, more alone than ever...

186   INT. 1961, EDWARD'S SUBURBAN HOUSE, BEDROOM - MORNING   186

Edward, in his bedroom, silently getting dressed... The PHONE
RINGS. He goes into STUDY to get it, letting it ring 5 times.

                         EDWARD
                 Hello.

A187   INT. 1961, AN OLD MOSCOW HOTEL - NIGHTFALL   A187

We see Arch Cummings, on phone, smoking, in a threadbare hotel
room. Out the window is a RED STAR, lit on top of the Kremlin.

                         ARCH CUMMINGS
                 I'm sorry, Edward...Mr. Mironov was
                 careless. He didn't learn how to hide
                 in plain sight. I truly did like
                 you... In another world we actually
                 would have been quite good friends...

B187   INT. 1961, EDWARD'S HOME, THE STUDY, VIRGINIA - MORNING B187

Edward on phone, in his study. He doesn't say anything...

                         ARCH CUMMINGS
                 Are you still there, Mother?

                         EDWARD
                 I'm here.

C187   INT. 1961, THE MOSCOW HOTEL ROOM - NIGHTFALL   C187

                         ARCH CUMMINGS
                     (looks out the window)
                 It was really rather simple. My old
                 friends here were quite capable of
                 transporting me from right under your
                 friend's nose, and here i am in the
                 splendor of downtown Moscow...This is
                 the only country that truly
                 appreciates loyalty.

D187   INT. 1961, EDWARD'S HOME, THE STUDY, VIRGINIA - MORNING D187

Edward on the phone. He looks at the painting of the river
Arch did for him, hanging over his fireplace.

                                                        (CONTINUED)

D187   CONTINUED: D187

                    ARCH CUMMINGS'S VOICE (OVER)
                     (as if reading his mind)
             Edward, I have a confession to make. I
             actually painted the river for you. I
             was always quite fond of you...I'm
             sorry. I'm sorry.

Edward is still.

                    ARCH CUMMINGS
             Sometimes, Edward, as clever as we
             both might be, a painting is nothing
             more than a painting...

                    EDWARD
                     (after a beat)
             Your worst fear has come true.

E187   INT. 1961, THE MOSCOW HOTEL ROOM - NIGHTFALL   E187

                    ARCH CUMMINGS
             What was that?

F187   INT. 1961, EDWARD'S HOME, THE STUDY, VIRGINIA - MORNING F187

                    EDWARD
             Alone and friendless, without a
             country of your own.

And Edward quietly hangs up.

G187   INT. 1961, THE MOSCOW HOTEL ROOM - NIGHTFALL   G187

Arch hangs up. He goes to stand by window in the shadow of the
Kremlin's red star, alone and friendless, without a country...

H187   INT. 1961, EDWARD'S HOME, THE STUDY, VIRGINIA - MORNING H187

187   Edward hasn't moved, staring at the painting. He gets up, 187
         takes it down, like so many things in his life...

191   OMIT SCENES 187-190   191

191   EXT. 1961, MOSCOW - AFTERNOON   191

John Russell, in winter coat, with groceries, crosses a quiet
street. Car suddenly comes around a corner and runs him over,
driving off. John Russell, lying in the milk from a broken
milk bottle, his blood turning the milk red...

192   INT. 1961, THE CITY BUS - EARLY MORNING   192

Edward rides to work, nearly indistinguishable from other
riders, reading their newspapers on their way to work.

193   OMITTED   193

A194   INT. A BASEMENT IN RUSSIAN PRISON - NIGHT   A194

Valentin is led by two Russian prison guards through a
basement hall.

                                                        (CONTINUED)

A194   CONTINUED: A194

And as he walks down the dark hall, a shadow emerges from a
doorway, and shoots Valentin in the back of the head...

194   INT. 1961, THE CITY BUS - MORNING   194

Edward peers through glasses at Personals: "Planning Wedding.
Will you attend?" He looks out the bus window and comes face to
face with his own reflection. And as he looks at himself...

195   EXT. 1961, A WASHINGTON STREET- MORNING   195

The Bus comes to a stop. Passengers get off... Edward moves
along his route, then turns into an old Victorian Building.

196   INT. 1961, THE SMITHSONIAN, WASHINGTON - MORNING   196

A class of children sit listening to a children's concert as
Edward walks through the museum, looking at exhibits. He
stops at a capsule that sent a monkey into orbit. A figure's
come to stand beside him... Stas, with a cup of coffee,
Tartar nearby. Brocco stands across the hall.

                    STAS SIYANKO
              (meaning the exhibit,
               ironic)
              We have a whole new place to fight
              over. The stars.

                    EDWARD
              Your offer. I have to decline... You
              have succeeded in stopping us from
              taking back Cuba. The damage is
              done... There is no need for you to
              put my son in danger... Let's leave it
              between you and me...

Stas is quiet, weighing the possibilities...

                    STAS SIYANKO
              Very well. I will wait. But there will
              come a time, when I will ask you to
              help me with a problem that wouldn't
              cost you much, but be of some value to
              me. After all, enemies can be friends
              and friends, enemies. You never know
              what the future will bring!

Edward doesn't say anything.

                    STAS
              This girl... Neither of us can really
              be sure about her. It's a question of
              trust. But if she means something to
              you, I wouldn't do anything to her...
              Because she is about to be apart of
              your family...I believe in family.

Edward is silent.

                    STAS (CONT'D)
              You want her to be apart of your
              family, don't you?

                                                        (CONTINUED)

196   CONTINUED:

Edward still doesn't say anything.

                    STAS (CONT'D)
          Then she is of no value to us.
          Whatever happens, happens.

                    EDWARD
          We wouldn't do something like that.

                    STAS
               (ironic)
          No, we wouldn't do something like
          that.

Stas looks down...

                    STAS (CONT'D)
          Your shoe, mother. It seems to be
          untied.

Edward looks down at his shoe. He hesitates for a moment,
then bends down, tightening his laces, the deal done...They
look at each other and move towards the exit.

                    STAS SIYANKO
          It was good to see you. We will talk
          again, my dear "friend."

The Tartar quietly comes to Stas's side.

                    THE TARTAR
               (In Russian)
          I'm buying a small souvenir for my
          Daughter.

The Tartar turns to a small SOUVENIR STAND...

                    THE TARTAR (CONT'D)
               (to Edward)
          I am sorry to bother... I only have a
          twenty dollar bill... they don't seem
          to have change...?

                    EDWARD
          Here...

He takes from his wallet a DOLLAR BILL with a pen mark on it.

                    EDWARD (CONT'D)
               (Wry)
          A gift with regards from the United
          States Government...

He gives him the dollar and Tartar pays for his souvenir.

                    THE TARTAR
          You are a very generous man.

                    STAS SIYANKO
               (A thin smile)
          Americans are always generous.

Stas starts to go, the Tartar at his side...

                         THE TARTAR
                For my little girl. Isn't it lovely?

He shows him a SNOW GLOBE of the Capital Building, the same
snow globe Edward Jr. showed his father years ago. Stas, not
interested, nods as they exit... Edward looks at Brocco.
They exchange a subtle look. Edward looks back at Stas, his
Tartar at his side... The Tartar turned into a mole, a
stranger Edward has planted in Stas's house. As Stas goes out
one way, stopping to help a woman with a baby carriage down
some steps, Edward goes out the other...

197   INT. 1961, EDWARD'S OFFICE, THE CIA - NIGHT   197

Edward in his office, a few boxes here and there, packing away
a ship in a bottle into a box carefully. Ray comes in...

                         RAY BROCCO
                I'm going home.

Edward nods, preoccupied.

                         EDWARD
                Is there anything else you can think
                of we will need.

                         RAY BROCCO
                We should have everything we need.

                         EDWARD
                   (looks up)
                The world's about to become a very
                different place. There will be new
                enemies. New rules.

Ray nods. Edward lowers his head. Ray starts to go, then slows.

                         RAY BROCCO
                My grandchild had a school project...
                To tell the class about what their
                grandparents did for a living...She
                asked me to come to school to tell the
                class what I do...I told her I
                couldn't... She wanted to know why. I
                told her I do very special work that
                nobody can know about. She asked my
                brother, who sells shoes to come and
                talk to the class about his work. He
                brought them different kinds of shoes
                to look at.

He's quiet. Edward, his head down. Ray shrugs, accepting
it's part of the job. He looks around the office for a last
time. As he starts to go, a sadness comes over him...

                         RAY BROCCO (CONT'D)
                The last one to leave please turn off
                the lights.

                                                    (CONTINUED)

197   CONTINUED: 197

                              EDWARD
                         (looks up)
                    What was that?

                              RAY BROCCO
                    I said don't forget to turn off the
                    lights.

WHEN WE HEAR CHURCH BELLS RING:

199   OMITTED   199

        EXT. 1961, A SMALL AFRICAN AIRFIELD, THE CONGO - DAY

        MIRIAM, her wedding dress in thin tissue paper over her arm, a
        suitcase at feet, says affectionate goodbye's to friends and
        family. She gets on SMALL PLANE, which taxies away, taking off.

200   INT. 1961, LEOPOLDVILLE APARTMENT, THE CONGO - DAY   200

        Edward Jr. happily shows Clover his tuxedo. No longer with
        Edward, she has found her peace... A KNOCK. Edward Jr., still
        talking, goes to get it... Edward stands at the door. An
        awkward moment, but it's his wedding day, and all's forgiven.

                              EDWARD JR.
                    I didn't expect you.

                              EDWARD
                    Do you think I'd miss your wedding day?

                              EDWARD JR.
                    Please come in...

        Edward comes in to see Clover already there.

                              CLOVER
                    Edward.

                              EDWARD
                    Margaret.

                              CLOVER
                    Please, sit down.

                              EDWARD
                    How was your flight over?

                              CLOVER
                    Long.

        Edward smiles.

                              EDWARD JR.
                    I'll get the champagne. Let's
                    celebrate.

                              EDWARD
                    How do you like living in Phoenix?

                                                    (CONTINUED)

                              CLOVER
                    Very much. It's the first time in
                    years I've been able to sleep...
                    There's nothing but desert and stars.

That says all. Edward Jr. comes out with a bottle of
champagne. He pops the cork, putting aside their differences,
and pours them each a glass of champagne.

                              CLOVER (CONT'D)
                    To your happiness.

                              EDWARD
                    To your happiness.

And as they drink to his happiness...

201   INT. 1961, THE SMALL PLANE, THE CONGO - DAY   201

Miriam, wedding dress on lap, flies in plane. PILOT and CO-
PILOT, two expressionless African men wearing reflecting
aviator sunglasses. The Co-Pilot gets up and pushes open her
door. She screams. As Pilot flies the plane, unconcerned, in
reflection of Co-Pilot's sunglasses, Miriam is overpowered.

202   EXT. 1961, THE SMALL PLANE, THE CONGO - DAY   202

Miriam, her body falling, still clutching her wedding dress,
suitcase thrown out after her, comes open, articles of
clothing scattering... The wedding dress comes out of her
hands, floating away...in the peaceful African sky.

203   EXT. 1961, THE ANGLICAN CHURCH, LEOPOLDVILLE - DAY   203

Edward Jr., holding a box with a yellow corsage, raising an
umbrella, Clover alongside him. Edward Jr. starts for the
church, but sees his father coming towards him. Edward Jr.
stops. Something is terribly wrong.

                              EDWARD
                    The Russians... The Russians had your
                    wife killed...

Edward Jr. drops the corsage. It looks like he can't stand
up. Edward reaches to hold him... Edward Jr. quietly
anguishing, his father whispering to him like a small child,
"shhhh..." Edward Jr.'s head pressed to his father's cheek...

                              CLOVER
                         (can barely speak)
                    What did you do?

Edward is quiet.

                              CLOVER (CONT'D)
                    What in God's name did you do?
                    Sweetheart?

She turns to her son...

203   CONTINUED: 203

                              EDWARD JR.
                    Go inside mother. Please go into the
                    church.

          She listens, going into the church. Edward is left holding
          his son on the street. And his son has to know...

                              EDWARD JR. (CONT'D)
                    Father? Did you have anything to do
                    with this?

                              EDWARD
                    No...No...No.

                              EDWARD JR.
                    She was pregnant, father. We were
                    going to have a child.

          Edward is dead still, ashen. Even he isn't prepared for this.

                              EDWARD
                    How do you know? They have Russian
                    doctors. They will tell you anything.

                              EDWARD JR.
                    I heard the heartbeat. It was your
                    grandchild.

          Edward is motionless. His son's tears and the rain dampen his
          shoulder. And Edward says, holding him close...

                              EDWARD
                    I am so sorry. I would never do
                    anything to hurt you.

          Tears run down his cheeks. As Edward holds him, we look into
          his son's eyes, and see no matter what he's been told, he knows
          the truth, who did this, and what the future holds... As people
          push by them for the bus, the church bell rings for a wedding.

204   INT. 1961 EDWARD'S SUBURBAN HOUSE, STUDY - EARLY MORNING 204

          Classical music plays on radio as Edward dresses for work. He
          comes down hall, stops, and goes into Study. He unlocks desk
          drawer with a key. He takes out an old envelope that has a
          child's fingerprints of blood. He breaks the seal and reads his
          father's suicide note for the first time: "THEY ARE RIGHT WHAT
          THEY SAY ABOUT ME. I WAS WEAK. A COWARD. I COMPROMISED MYSELF.
          MY HONOR. MY FAMILY. MY COUNTRY. I AM ASHAMED OF MYSELF. TO MY
          WIFE, I AM SORRY I HAVE DONE THIS TO YOU. TO MY SON, I HOPE YOU
          WILL GROW TO BE A COURAGEOUS MAN. A GOOD HUSBAND. A GOOD
          FATHER. I HOPE WHATEVER YOU DECIDE TO DO, YOU LEAD A GOOD FULL
          LIFE. I HOPE WHATEVER YOUR DREAMS MAY BE, COME TRUE." Edward
          quietly holds the letter, then lights a match to it, throwing
          it in a trash bin to burn. The radio finishes its classical
          music program. A show called "The Morning Sermon" starts. The
          preacher reads from the bible: "I am the Good Shepherd." "The
          Good Shepherd watches over his flock..."

205   EXT. 1961, EDWARD SUBURBAN HOUSE, VIRGINIA - EARLY MORNING 205

Edward, in raincoat, with briefcase, comes out, locking door.
He takes up the newspaper, and moves along in his familiar
posture, head down as if he had lost something....

206   EXT. 1961, THE CIA BUILDING, WASHINGTON - EARLY MORNING   206

Edward crosses the quiet street, going down the steps and
disappearing into the old government building. THE SERMON
ENDS...

207   INT. 1961, THE CIA BUILDING - EARLY MORNING   207

Edward in his office, looking out the window, stripped bare
of all its furniture, completely empty.

208   INT. 1961, EDWARD'S OFFICE, THE CIA - EARLY MORNING   208

A Security Officer standing next to a row of safes hands
Edward a sheet on a clipboard. Edward looks it over, then
signs the safes away. Movers begin to roll them down the
hall, and Edward slowly follows, disappearing down the long
hall.

AND THERE'S THE SOUND OF A KETTLE DRUM...

209   INT. 1939, THE YALE THEATRE CLUB - DAY   209

Yale stage. An ORCHESTRA PLAYING. Miss Buttercup, young and
vibrant, filled with hope, moving around the stage, singing.

                    BUTTERCUP
        "For I'm called little Buttercup --
        dear little Buttercup, though I could
        never tell why... But still I'm called
        'Buttercup --' poor little Buttercup,
        sweet little Buttercup, I...!"

                                    FADE OUT:

Q&A WITH ERIC ROTH

If Eric Roth had run off to a desert island in 1994, he would still be known as the Academy Award–winning writer of *Forrest Gump*—both a film and a phenomenon of the 1990s. Not only was *Gump* a commercial success, but several of the film's lines, such as "Life is like a box of chocolates" or "Run, Forrest! Run!" were repeated—or parodied—by every element of popular culture.

Many writers would be tempted to duplicate the characters and themes that created such a success, but Roth has consistently challenged himself to write movies that stand out among the never-ending sequels offered by Hollywood studios. In 1994, with *Gump* still playing in theaters, he started to write *The Good Shepherd*, a gripping story of one man's life that is intertwined with the formation of the CIA.

For the past 12 years, Roth has worked to get *The Good Shepherd* produced. During that period, he has also been involved with a wide variety of notable films, becoming known both for adaptations of novels and original screenplays that dramatize the issues of our time. He wrote the first draft of the apocalyptic film *The Postman* (1997). A year later, he and Richard La Gravanese adapted Nicholas Evans' romantic novel, *The Horse Whisperer* (1998). After reading *The Good Shepherd*, writer/director Michael Mann contacted Roth and they wrote *The Insider* (1999), the true story of a tobacco industry whistleblower and his relationship with a *60 Minutes* producer. *The Insider* was

This is an expanded version of an article by Mark Lee that was initially published in the December 2006 issue of *Written By, The Magazine of the Writers Guild of America, West*. Q&A copyright © 2007 by Mark Lee. Reprinted by permission. Mark Lee, the author of the novel *The Lost Tribe*, has written six produced plays and two produced screenplays.

nominated for seven Academy awards and won the Humanitas Prize in 2000 for best feature film screenplay. Roth and Mann followed this success with *Ali* (2001)—a sprawling biopic about the legendary boxer. Last year, Roth and Tony Kushner received co-credit for the controversial film *Munich*.

Sitting down for an interview, Eric Roth is relaxed and unpretentious. It's not surprising to find out that he likes to spend his spare time at the race-track figuring out the chances for long-shot horses. But when he talks about writing, Roth's casual manner disappears. He leans forward and speaks rapidly.

Q: *I can still remember when my brother and I opened up a cardboard box in the attic and discovered that my father was in the OSS, the predecessor of the CIA. It was difficult for us to reconcile the father who cut the lawn and built a treehouse with the man who blew up bridges and arranged attacks on Japanese soldiers.* The Good Shepherd *evoked the same kind of response from me. It dramatizes the change from the American idealism of World War II into the cynicism of espionage during the Cold War era. It's both an early history of the CIA and a dramatization of a turning point in American history. Eric, when you decide to write something inspired by history, it's easy for a writer to be overcome by details. Where do you start? With characters, incidents, an idea of what you want to say?*

ERIC ROTH: I normally start with a theme as to what the movie might be about, and then I draw the characters and then the situations from that. *The Good Shepherd* is about how one rectifies their own sort of moral values with bigger issues. It's difficult, of course, to put a theme into one sentence, but the film in a certain sense is about trust—and what secrecy does to people. There are approximately thirty thousand people involved in America's intelligence community. So I asked myself, "Well, what is the fiction of this within the reality?" In other words, who are the people that were involved in the CIA? Where did they come from? And what did they become? And I found some people who fit some ideas I would like to express and some people that didn't. So I wrapped the lead character that Matt Damon plays [Edward Wilson] around three or four real people. But my interpretation of them is a pure fiction, so that it's a fiction based on the realities of several people.

So you started writing The Good Shepherd *with a theme and some real-life characters based on your research and then—*

ER: —then you write *Fade In*. In my scripts, I've always known what the opening is going to be and the ending. And I can't think of any movie of mine that's ever been made that was created differently. [The producers] always maintained the opening and the ending. The middle's a big blank and I let the character take me along on that journey. Now with *The Good Shepherd*, it's a little more confined because I was trying to write to certain historical events. Some people who have seen the movie or read the script felt that I rewrote things to accommodate today's history, but I wrote this script twelve years ago. Certain things hold true over a period of time.

When I read The Good Shepherd, *I assumed that your lead character, Edward Wilson, was based on James Jesus Angleton, the CIA's first director for counterintelligence. Like your protagonist, Angleton went to Yale, he worked in London during the war, and had the CIA codename "Mother."*

ER: Angleton is a unique individual. He's in some ways quite different from the Edward Wilson character and in some ways very similar. He was very smart. I don't want to use this too pejoratively, but I think he knew better. In other words, I made my lead character slightly more innocent than maybe Angleton really was. For almost thirty-five years, Angleton was the main source of power in the agency because everything went through his hands.

James Angleton became fairly paranoid towards the end of his career and started to believe that a number of famous people—including Gerald Ford and Henry Kissinger—were Soviet agents.

ER: Right.

In The Good Shepherd *you don't really focus on that paranoia as much as your character's loss of innocence.*

ER: I'm not sure that "innocence" is even the right word. I think it's about what we talked about a little bit earlier… about a sort of morality. The CIA does have some idealistic people who have done good things to protect our country. But some people have abused their power.

In The Good Shepherd *you set several scenes on Deer Island, which is a real location in the middle of the St. Lawrence River, a private resort owned by Skull and Bones. The members bring their eligible daughters there for a weekend so that they can meet and ostensibly breed with—*

ER: —the next generation.

You're able to take this real-life location and then use it to develop your characters. Here Edward Wilson meets a young woman named Clover who eventually becomes his wife. So does the fact come first, then you think up a scene? Or do you think up the scene and then find a location from the historical record?

ER: I knew that I wanted Wilson to end up with somebody who is from that society, so that decision came first. I also knew from more recent history that there was a place—Bohemian Grove out here in San Francisco—that was sort of the western version of Deer Island. So then I did a little research as to where the Skull and Bones people might have gone and I discovered the location. So it's just a perfect setting for where Wilson could meet a friend's sister.

The story is very definitely framed within a particular context, which is the failure of the Bay of Pigs invasion, and a hunt for a possible traitor who betrayed that expedition. How did you make the choice that you're going to use in a sense the Bay of Pigs as a framing device?

ER: I was interested in the formation of the CIA. And I think that the CIA changed from 1961 on and then became drastically changed after the Vietnam War. If I kept going [forward in time], it would be another movie. The Bay of Pigs disaster was a good place to put a man who's under incredible pressure. In other words, it forces the character to look back and say, "How did I get to here?"

In your script, the lead character's family story and institutional story of the CIA seem to interweave throughout the story, and then both end up in the same place at the conclusion.

ER: The two strands come together in a tragic way. We see a man who helped write the rules for how the CIA was supposed to behave and then had to live with those rules whether he liked them or not. I don't want to give too much away about the movie, but I can tell you that Wilson's son goes into the CIA and there are consequences from that.

When you write, do you think of your story in a linear way? Obviously The Good Shepherd *is not a linear screenplay.*

ER: It's linear in its own way.

But did you outline the story with one historical incident following another?

ER: I don't outline very often because I think it takes all the mystery out of it, the fun out of [the writing process]. By not outlining, you don't know quite where you're going to go. *The Good Shepherd* is a little different because there are certain events you want to cover, but the middle part was a blank to me. I'll outline two or three scenes ahead and that's it. I know that other writers use different techniques—cards and boards and things like that. But I find it too restricting for me. Sometimes, the lack of an outline causes me to go down the wrong road and then I have to come back. But I can usually catch it because every day of the week, I go back to page one.

So, in effect, you're continually rewriting.

ER: Yeah. It's not that my scripts are better or worse than anybody else's, but they might be a little further along because during the year I've worked on them, I've gone through the equivalent of maybe four or five rewrites.

And do you write every day?

ER: Every day except … well, weekends, sometimes, you know. I usually write four hours a day, and then at night. I find I can be creative from about eight until noon. And then I dick around or play with the kids or go to the races. And then at night I usually [resume] around nine o'clock. And I used to go pretty late, but I'm too old now.

You've written a fair amount of scripts during your career. Have you ever had writer's block?

ER: Never. I've had projects that don't work and others that have taken me a long time to finish. The one piece of advice I give at writer's conferences is: "Just change the weather when you get in trouble." In other words, make it rain, and all of a sudden you look at it very differently.

Raymond Chandler once wrote, "When in doubt, have a man come through a door with a gun in his hand."

ER: Maybe I've had writer's block and I didn't know it, but I never had … I don't really have that fear. Maybe I'm just lucky. Obviously, like everyone, I do have a fear of rejection, but maybe my gambler's mentality has helped me deal with that. In addition, I've had children and people around me who I've loved and who have loved me for a long time, so what's the worst that can happen? If I fail, I'll go do something else … drive a taxi.

You started writing documentary films when you were a graduate student at UCLA.

ER: Right. A group of us did a film in 1968 about the Poor People's March on Washington that was fairly well received.

So how did you make the transition to writing a movie screenplay?

ER: Once again, I used a real event. There was an antiwar radical at the time named Jerry Rubin and he was in jail in Santa Rosa, California, but for probably opening his mouth once too often—you know, causing trouble. But then the authorities made him one of the defendants in what eventually was called the "Chicago Seven" trial. These seven activists were accused of creating a "conspiracy" during the Democratic Convention. For some reason, the attorney general's office was afraid of putting Jerry Rubin on an airplane, so they drove him across the country in a car with a murderer and a bank robber who they were extraditing to Chicago.

What a great idea for a screenplay!

ER: That's what I thought. I started wondering: *What's this road trip like? Two FBI agents and these three guys in the same car.* I happened to have known the activist Abby Hoffman fairly well at the time, so I found out a few things that happened and invented the rest. The screenplay won the Samuel Goldwyn Writing Award in 1970 and that helped me get an agent. Actually, I won the award alongside a guy named Colin Higgins, who went on to write *Harold and Maude* and *Nine to Five.* Colin was a wonderful human being who died way too young. I still miss him.

Can screenwriting be taught? These days, there's an entire industry of screenwriting seminars and how-to books.

ER: You can be taught the form. I think you can probably learn dramatic structures. But at some point, writing needs to become instinctive to you. You need to be brave enough to express yourself and, as I say, brave enough to fail. I find it hard to judge other writers. People send me screenplays and I can never tell you if it's good, bad, or indifferent. The only thing I tell you when I read someone else's screenplay is how I would do it, but that doesn't necessarily mean that it's right. Getting back to the practical aspects of being a screenwriter, the biggest thing is to get an agent and to just keep writing. You have to try to find a distinctive voice for your characters and then a voice for yourself.

The Good Shepherd *took a long time to get made. You wrote the screenplay twelve years ago. I read that it was initially inspired by Norman Mailer's novel* Harlot's Ghost.

ER: Well, not that it was inspired so much, but the novel dovetailed with my own interest in this. I started to think about the screenplay right after *Forrest*

Gump won the Academy Award. Some studios came to me and said: "What would you like to do?" I think they assumed I was going to write something in the fantasy realm or…

Forrest Gump, *Part Two.*

ER: Right. But I wanted to do this serious subject matter, which was something that interested me. And it turned out that Francis Coppola had some sort of involvement with *Harlot's Ghost.* So I went to him and said, "I would really like to write about this subject matter." And he said, "Let's do it. Give me a great script." I went away for a year and wrote the screenplay. For various reasons, it didn't work out with Francis, but we've remained close and he's now the film's executive producer.

How did the script evolve over the twelve-year period before it was produced? Did you change the characters or the structure?

ER: The characters didn't change very much. But one change came from a person who was involved with the project for a while—Phil Kaufman—who's a wonderful director. The original script was linear, even though it was based on one flashback—we saw a man getting dressed to go somewhere. It turned out at the end of the movie that he's going to a funeral, but everything from that point on is a flashback.

But as you worked with Phil Kaufman…?

ER: We discussed the possibility of making it go back and forth in time. We had a story being told in 1961 as to who gave away the secret about invading the Bay of Pigs. We decided to focus on a central character responsible for that action, and then we looked back on his life and discovered how he got to that place.

So the crucial change was that the revised script moved back and forth between 1961 and the incidents that shaped Edward Wilson's life.

ER: Correct. Of course some scenes fell by the wayside, like they normally will—some things I wish still existed—but nothing I think that significant disappeared. The script really stayed basically the same.

Does that make The Good Shepherd *an unusual project for you?*

ER: I've been fortunate; I have a lot of movies made. But I found that in the long run, the essence of my original vision hasn't been changed that much during the development process. Obviously, there have been battles with directors about how a scene should go or vice versa. But the basic idea stays the same. I think one of the reasons for this is that I spend a lot of time writing my screenplays, so if someone's going to get involved they usually buy into the theme and the subject matter and the characters.

Usually, when a screenplay engenders a great success, the people with money ask you to write something that's "the same…only different." After you won the Academy Award for Forrest Gump, *you went against that tendency and wrote* The Good Shepherd.

ER: I always want to do something that challenges me. It's like in bridge—you know, bid bold and go down. That being said, I don't know if I could have written another *Forrest Gump*. I couldn't. That film was some kind of alchemy that I had something to do with, and nothing to do with.

One of the more interesting aspects of your screenplay for Forrest Gump *is the way you've changed the tone of Winston's Groom's novel. In the novel, Forrest does not marry Jenny, and Jenny does not die of AIDS. In the screenplay, Forrest is innocent and kind, whereas in the novel he's somewhat of a more cynical character.*

ER: The novel was fun, but it was a little farcical for my taste. The good news for me when I first read the novel was that—at that point—nobody was really interested in the project. A few other writers had tried different approaches and the studio couldn't have cared less about it. I had the freedom to create anything. So I said, "Let's start from scratch." For whatever reason, I placed Forrest on the bench and had the feather and all this stuff. Somehow I saw it all as this wonderful fable. The interesting thing about that movie is that the absurd stuff about presidents getting shot or all the ironies of our existence during that time period are really more fabulous than the life stuff. They're scenes that you couldn't invent.

Incidents like the Ping Pong tournament that helped normalize our relationship with China?

ER: Yes. I approached Forrest Gump like every one of my characters. I took him as a real person and said, "What if a real guy existed who lived in this situation?" And then I do have sometimes a sense of irony. And Bob Zemeckis, the director, had a healthy sense of cynicism. The film sort of poked a stick in a lot of people's eyes. That's why there was this debate: Is it liberal? Is it right-wing? I don't think it's any of those things. *Forrest Gump* is an equal opportunity sort of knocker in the sense that every-body—and everything—is up for evaluation. And then there's this one guy who is sort of drifting along through life who ends up in these seminal moments.

So you feel that your crucial decision in the screenplay was deciding to regard Forrest as a real person?

ER: That, and a few other things. There's a sadness and loneliness in my screenplays, and I don't know why because I'm not generally a very sad person. But I think there is. That's what Tom Hanks has said about my work, and a bunch of other people: "Why are your characters always so sad or lonely?" Along with that, I'm always moved by the time passing. I think it has to do with trying to hold on to moments as they disappear. Bob Zemeckis said something that I think is very smart about *Gump*: one of the successes of the film was that it gave an audience permission to grieve together about the time passing. You could think the movie is silly or disagree with the politics, but nobody could dispute the fact that they were once nineteen and then they were thirty-nine and then they're forty-nine. There's a joy to it too, but there's a sadness about just the passage of time, about our youth going. And it's the thing that's always appealed to me about movies in general. I mean, when I think about it, just off the top of my head, *To Kill a Mockingbird* reminds me of the summer. It's just this sort of gray period of being a child. Some movies can go into your psyche and into your subliminal dream life.

That line of sadness that runs through your work can be subtle, but very powerful. For me, one of the most emotionally powerful scenes in your screenplay for The Insider *shows a husband walking over to a kitchen sink and washing his hands in it, even though his wife tells him…*

ER: …not to.

But he ends up doing it anyway. The scene is very compressed, it seems like a small moment, but it's so immensely sad because you're revealing the end of a marriage.

ER: That one may have been actually out of life because I've been through a divorce. It wasn't that my ex-wife didn't want me to wash my hands in the sink, but that just seemed like a good representation of that. I don't know where that came from, you know, but it just did.

But there's no formula for a great scene. You can't create it with a computer.

ER: All I hope for with each new project is that I'm lucky enough to get a challenge. And I was lucky in a way because I'm sort of a gambler. I like to play the horses and that kind of thing. If you're willing to gamble as a writer, then you take a chance on a lot of different things. And the worst that happens is they're not going to like it and you failed. But at least I failed on my own terms: I gave it my best shot.

Every screenwriter who has been working for a while has a closet filled with unproduced scripts. Written By's *annual issue of unproduced work gets a flood of submissions.*
ER: The biggest lesson I've learned over the years is patience. Things seem to come around if they're worthy, despite the fact of all the vagaries of the business. *The Good Shepherd* is certainly an example of that.

I've read that the script led to one of your most productive relationships, with director/writer Michael Mann. Is it true that he read The Good Shepherd *and decided that he wanted you to write about Jeffrey Wigand, the tobacco industry whistleblower?*
ER: That's the project that eventually began *The Insider.*

When you read The Insider, *you realize that there isn't a great deal of action, but somehow you've been able to turn the film into a thriller. It's a thriller about men talking on the phones and meeting in hotel rooms.*
ER: Both Michael Mann and I are interested in what happens to men under pressure. We're interested in the kind of moral decisions people have to make in unusual circumstances. There's a "cheat" in *The Insider*, but it's not the thriller aspect. What you learn in Screenplay 101 is that you're supposed to show rather than tell, but there's a lot of telling in *The Insider.*

If you look at the movie or read the script, you'll see that there's certain scenes where we literally told the audience what we want to accomplish, but somehow we managed to do it in a way that made it seem fresh and sounded like they were real conversations that people were having. This was a little premeditated and it's not normally the way I like to write. I try to be a little more instinctive.

There's another aspect of the film that is very instructive for any screenwriter. The Insider *is very clever about the selective introduction of information. It's not so obvious that you're giving out facts because you're revealing them slowly—one piece at a time. The film breaks down into two separate tensions:* What is this man's secret? *And then,* What will happen to him when he reveals the secret?
ER: I don't care if you write comedy, if you write action movies, drama— all the laws of drama apply. I don't care how postmodern you get with it. I

don't care if you bring in fantasy elements, everything still has three, maybe four acts. What story are you telling? Who are you telling the thing about? What's the story going to be? You have to bring in some kind of complications in the second act. And you have to resolve it with either catharsis or bring in a *deus ex machina*. And you can do this as interesting as you want or not.

But isn't there a different feeling creating a screenplay like The Insider *where—because of legal constraints—every scene pretty much has to be as truthful as possible? In* The Good Shepherd *you were able to use fictionalized characters.*

ER: Well, there's some similarity and obviously some differences. Michael Mann and I were under very tight reins when we created *The Insider* because the characters were very real people.

When the film came out 60 Minutes *correspondent Mike Wallace was said to be unhappy with the way he was portrayed.*

ER: Michael and I were not creating a documentary. But on the other hand, I think there's an obligation that I don't slander the man. In other words, I want to be fair—and ethical—but I also have to be passionate about the screenplay because that's part of the fun of writing.

The contrast between the real-life person and the character he inspired must have been especially strong when you and Michael Mann wrote the screenplay for Ali. *In this case, you're dramatizing the life of an individual who is also truly legendary.*

ER: This was a tough one. And I don't know if we succeeded altogether. It's difficult because Mohammed Ali is such a huge personality that only one person could be him. And secondly, they also had made a pretty wonderful movie about Ali as a documentary. So once again, Michael and I tried to say what was interesting to Ali. And fortunately I got to meet him, spend time with him. There's a lot written about Ali that probably you could write it better than I could have ever said it. So on one hand we wanted to tell his story; on the other hand we don't want to tell a biography. We set out to dramatize the things that interested us about a guy. How it felt to be under that kind of pressure–trying to fulfill his own dreams as he carries the world on your shoulder in that way. Ali had enough ego, narcissism, all those things, and intelligence, and street smarts, but also a great deal of responsibility.

The film Ali *raises some fascinating issues for writers today in that there is a clear difference between the theatrical version and the so-called director's cut on DVD. Mann took out twenty minutes of the theatrical version and put in thirty minutes of unseen footage. So in the future, is there going to be a director's cut of* The Good Shepherd?

ER: There is, definitely. I know for a fact there's actually going to probably be a four-hour director's cut. In a way, I'm hoisted on my own petard because I probably write too much, even though I know that you can't normally make four-hour movies. I guess I have a novelistic approach to some extent, which may or may not be compatible with filmmaking. But I found that the movies have been as long or as short as directors have wanted them to be. The length issue makes you compress and think up scenes that fit the movie form.

Reading your produced screenplays and teleplays, I could see a consistent theme through-out your work. You seem to be interested in the moral and personal "costs" of the decisions we make in our lives. Most recently in Munich *[co-written by Tony Kushner], you tried to show how violence touches the lives of men who volunteer to avenge an act of terrorism. Some critics of* Munich *felt that Israeli agents don't routinely have doubts about their duty, but you and Kushner were going for something deeper.*

ER: I can't speak for Israeli agents, but this was material that I was lucky enough to have Stephen Spielberg give to me and say: "Let's see how well we can do." *Munich* was attributed to be a real story about some real people that supposedly did have doubts. I felt that it was at least my version of this—that it was important that we recognize that as human beings, I think we all have some doubts and we may not show them. So some people drink and some people beat their wives and some people rob banks and some people become depressed. In other words, there are other ways to exhibit your doubts. I don't care how crazy you are—some reaction is going to happen. In situations described in *Munich,* people are doing what they think is the right thing. And then they had to evaluate the reasons they were doing it.

It's clear that you approach a project like Munich *or* The Good Shepherd *with a great deal of passion for these characters and themes. In that situation, should you write the legendary two-hundred-page screenplay putting in everything that you feel?*

ER: Quite honestly I don't know the answer to that because I don't want to write a two-hundred-page screenplay. I think that that's impractical. Never mind whether it's the right or wrong thing to do. You are starting to kill your-self before you've even started; in other words, there is a self-censorship we need to have, or at least self-criticism. My screenplays are a little bit longer than usual because that's just my style of writing. I have a lot of prose. If you took the prose out, it would cut the screenplays incredibly. You know, it's funny. I get criticized for the lengths; on the other hand, they say, "We love these scripts because we can see what the movie looks like." And the reason they can see what the movie looks like is because I write out to a certain extent a lot of detail, a lot of description, because I think God's in the details. I like to give sort of the sense of what I would like an actor to feel about what he's saying.

The writer doesn't just invent a story—he or she creates a world.

ER: Each script is so different. I think that *The Good Shepherd* could have been my best work. We'll have to see if that's true. Someone else has to judge that. For me, I'm more than pleased and proud of it. You sit in that room alone and then it becomes a piece of celluloid and you hope that it's everything you wanted it to be. When I get an assignment or I come up with an idea, I think, "Look how great this is! I get to go now and be a pirate or whatever." I don't think about success or failure or whatever. I just want it to be as best as I can do it.

And then you sit down and write the script.

ER: When I write "Fade Out," at least I'm happy with it for that ten minutes. And then, you know, you start reevaluating the whole thing— how you screwed it all up. I think I still have a certain drive to want to be respected and be successful—not in a money sense so much, even though I like having a good living and a good life. But you want other people to respect the ideas there, to think that there's something to be said that's interesting, to be moved by it. I mean, maybe it sounds like a cliché, but there's nothing better to me than to go sit in a movie theater with an audience and see them laugh and cry or be thoughtful.

That's one advantage that a screenwriter or a playwright has over a novelist. You can't watch someone read a book and then stop him or her and ask, "Why did you smile reading that last page?"

ER: I was at one of the previews of *The Good Shepherd*. And I'm not even going to tell you whether the audience liked or disliked the movie. But they sat there and didn't move a muscle for two-and-a-half hours. Now they were at least fascinated, you know? That was real success for me.

Do you think, in terms of the role of the screenwriter, it has changed in the last few years?

ER: Despite what everybody else seem to feel, I think that the writer has gained more respect. For a brief period of time it seemed like the screenwriter was kind of a rock star, in a bizarre way. I don't know where that came from. It was so odd, you know? Screenwriting is a hybrid of so many different things. It's not a play; it's not a novel. It's a combination of so many things. If you're a good craftsman it's nice to be respected, and you certainly can get your ideas across.

You have six children. Would you want them to be writers?

ER: Sure, I'd love that.

What advice would you give them at the start?

ER: I'd say, "Go for it!" I don't really like it when people are negative and say, "Well, you don't want go into the movie business." I think it's a wonderful gift to be able to write. You sort of get paid to go visit all these different worlds.

Do you think that technological change is affecting the kind of stories that people are writing? Is it changing film?

ER: I haven't found that. When I start writing a screenplay, I'm always asked to do the same things: Can you come up with a great love story? Can you come up with a great fantasy? Can you come up with...? No matter what changes, the stories are the same.

CAST AND CREW CREDITS

UNIVERSAL PICTURES and
MORGAN CREEK PRODUCTIONS
Present
An AMERICAN ZOETROPE Production
A TRIBECA Production

"THE GOOD SHEPHERD"

MATT DAMON   ANGELINA JOLIE   ALEC BALDWIN   TAMMY BLANCHARD   BILLY CRUDUP
ROBERT DE NIRO   KEIR DULLEA   MICHAEL GAMBON   MARTINA GEDECK   WILLIAM HURT
TIMOTHY HUTTON   MARK IVANIR   GABRIEL MACHT   LEE PACE   JOE PESCI
EDDIE REDMAYNE   JOHN SESSIONS   OLEG STEFAN   JOHN TURTURRO

Directed by
ROBERT DE NIRO

Written by
ERIC ROTH

Produced by
JAMES G. ROBINSON

Produced by
JANE ROSENTHAL
ROBERT DE NIRO

Executive Producers
FRANCIS FORD COPPOLA
DAVID ROBINSON

Executive Producers
HOWARD KAPLAN
GUY McELWAINE
CHRIS BRIGHAM

Director of Photography
ROBERT RICHARDSON, ASC

Production Designer
JEANNINE OPPEWALL

Editor
TARIQ ANWAR

Music by
MARCELO ZARVOS
BRUCE FOWLER

Music Supervisor
KATHY NELSON

Costume Designer
ANN ROTH

Casting by
AMANDA MACKEY, CSA
CATHY SANDRICH
GELFOND, CSA
SIG DE MIGUEL

Visual Effects Supervisor
ROB LEGATO

CAST

Edward Wilson . . . . Matt Damon
Clover / Margaret Russell . . . Angelina Jolie
Sam Murach . . . . Alec Baldwin
Laura . . . . Tammy Blanchard
Arch Cummings . . . . Billy Crudup
Senator Russell . . . . Keir Dullea
Dr. Fredericks . . . . Michael Gambon
Hanna Schiller . . . . . . Martina Gedeck
Philip Allen . . . . William Hurt
Thomas Wilson . . . . . Timothy Hutton
Valentin Mironov #2 . . . . . . Mark Ivanir
John Russell . . . . Gabriel Macht
Richard Hayes . . . . Lee Pace
Joseph Palmi . . . . Joe Pesci
Edward Wilson, Jr.. . . . . Eddie Redmayne
Valentin Mironov #1 / Yuri Modin
. . . . John Sessions
Ulysses / Stas Siyanko . . . . . Oleg Stefan
Ray Brocco . . . . John Turturro
Bill Sullivan . . . . Robert De Niro
Dollar Woman . . . . . Yelena Shmulenson
Dollar Little Boy . . . . Jack Martin

Philip Allen's Secretary . . Anne-Marie Cusson
Bay of Pigs Voiceover
. . . . Robert Bermudez Cordell
Spanish Translator . . . . David Crommett
Pinafore Actors . . . . Michael Arden
Justin Bohon
Justin Daniel
Michael Flanigan
John Hill
Will Reynolds
Michael Seelbach
Ryan Michael Shaw
HMS Pinafore Singer . . . . Stephen Powell
Bonesman / Boatswain . . . Henry Gummer
Dancing Skeleton . . . . . Gregory Marcel
Young Edward Wilson . . . Austin Williams
Connie Wilson . . . . Sophie Sutton
Mr. Haupt . . . . Lars Gerhard
Mr. Haupt's Translator . . . Tessa Keimes
Dr. Manheim . . . . Peter Kybart
Man At Jazz Club . . . . . . Rob Barnes
Mrs. John Russell, Sr. . . . . Lee Bryant
Toddy Allen . . . . Laila Robins

Older Bonesman 1940 . . Redman Maxfield
Reverend Collins . . . . . . John Whitehead
Deer Island Crooner 1940 . . . Jeff Skowron
John Russell, Jr.'s Girlfriend
. . . . Meredith Deacon
Army Man 1940 . . . . Josh Casaubon
Photography Technical Officer
. . . . Christopher Evan Welch
Sound Technical Officer . . . . Tuc Watkins
Tailor . . . . Leonard Logsdail
Tailor Shop Guard . . . . Eric Lindh
Cryptographers . . . . Trace Taylor
                               Amanda Barron
Lord Cooper . . . . James Faulkner
Cambridge Club Butler
. . . . Robert Ian MacKenzie
Herr Franck . . . . Dieter Riesle
Sasha / Tartar . . . . Sandor Tecsy
Edward Jr. (Ages 6-7) . . . . Tommy Nelson
Guard With Sullivan . . . . Greg Plitt
Dr. Ibanez . . . . Marcos Cohen
Michael Johnson . . . . Jeff Applegate
CIA Insect Man . . . . Jon Monett
Edward's Secretary . . . . . Sandee Conrad
Husband Dinner Guest
. . . . Jonathan Dokuchitz
Wife Dinner Guest . . . . . . Susan Haskell
Santa Claus . . . . Sjoerd deJong
Teletype Operations Officer . . . . Neal Huff
Teletype Communications Officer
. . . . Jason Butler Harner
Safe House Operations Officer
. . . . Amy Wright
Cherry Orchard Actor . . Matthew Humphreys
Cherry Orchard Actress . . . . Karron Graves
Laura's Taxi Driver . . . . Robert C. Kirk
"Dame" Bonesmen . . . . . . Reathel Bean
                               Jerry Coyle
                               Wally Dunn
                               Roger Rathburn
Piano Player . . . . Mike Melvoin
Telephone Operations Officer
. . . . Glenn Kalison
Technical Service Officer . . . . . John Knox
Bonesman 1960 . . . . . . Benjamin Eakeley
Palmi's Bodyguards . . . . . . Gino Cafarelli
                               Tommy DeVito
Tina Palmi . . . . Stefanie Nava
Palmi's Granddaughter . . . . Isabella Cimato
Palmi's Grandson . . . . . . Jimmy Marchese
Bonesman MC 1961 . . . . Robert Prescott
Reverend Christiansen . . . . . Bill McHugh
1961 Deer Island Singer
. . . . Ann Hampton Callway

FBI Agent . . . . . . Christopher Druckman
Miriam . . . . Liya Kebede
Philip Allen's Driver . . . . . . John Henry

Stunt Coordinators . . George Aguilar, John
   Cenatiempo, Stephen Pope, Paul Herbert
Stunts . . . . . . Aaron Vexler, Lloyd Bass,
   Chris Place, Andy Smart, April Washington,
   Levan Doran, Nancy J. LaRiviere, Roy Alon,
   Sally Hathaway, Douglas Crosby, Gerald L.
   Orange, Bill Anagnos, Jill Brown, Don
   Hewitt, Jeff Gibson, Jacob Williams, Al
   Cerullo, Michael Mancuso, Peter White,
   William Wright, Connor Sexton

CREW

Unit Production Manager . . Joseph E. Iberti
First Assistant Director . . . . H. H. Cooper
Second Assistant Director . Jennifer Truelove
Production Executive . . . . . Andy Fraser
Post Production Supervisor . . Jennifer Lane
CIA Technical Advisor . . . Milton Bearden
Camera Operator / Steadicam
. . . . Larry McConkey
First A Camera Assistant . . Gregor Tavenner
Second B Camera Assistant . . Xiomara Comrie
Camera Loaders . . . . Robyn Noble
                               Julien De La Cruz
Camera Production Assistant . . Hilary Benas
Video Assist . . . . Daniel R. Salk
Sound Mixer . . . . Tom Nelson
Boom Operator . . . . . . Frank Graziadei
Second Boom/Cable . . . . . Tommy Louie
Playback Mixer . . . . Jason Stasium
Production Music Mixer . . . Joseph Magee
Art Director . . . . Robert Guerra
Assistant Art Directors . . . . Edward Pisoni,
   Adam Scher, Barbra Matis, John Wright
      Stevens, Darrell Keister
Graphic Designers . . . . . Mark Bachman
                               Leo Holder
Art Department Coordinator . . Claire Kirk
Storyboard Artist . . . . John Davis
Set Decorators . . . Gretchen Rau, Leslie E.
      Rollins, Alyssa Winter
Assistant Set Decorators . . Alexandra Mazur
                               Harriet S. Zucker
On Set Dressers . . . . . . Ruth A. DeLeon
                               Steve Finkin
Set Dec Buyers . . . . Lisa Kent
                               Susan Raney
Set Dec Coordinator . . . . . Tina Khayat
Leadman . . . . Philip C. Canfield

Set Dressers . . . . Deborah Canfield,
Patrice Canfield-Longo, T. Kelly Canfield,
Richard Hoppe, Christopher Heaps,
Christopher Ferraro, Gus Pappadopolous,
William Canfield, Greco
Property Master . . . . Russell Bobbitt
NY Property Masters . . . . Anthony Dimeo
Joseph Badalucco, Jr.
Assistant Props . . . . . James P. McDonagh
Damian Costa
Gaffer . . . . Ian Kincaid
NY Gaffer . . . . Michael Burke
Rigging Gaffer . . . . Jimmy Dolan
Dimmer Board Operator . . Brooke Stanford
Best Boy Electric . . . . Jim Mah
Electrics . . Mike Price, Grady Bayersdorfer,
Kelly Rutkowski, Brian McClean, Tom
O'Connor
Generator Operators . . . . . Don Schreck
Rob Merck
Rigging Best Boy . . . . Richard N. Dolan
Rigging Electrics . . . Peter McEntyre, Brian
Stocklin, Charles Meeres III, Glynnis J.
Burke, Petr Hlinomaz, Jack Coffin, Jimmy
Walsh Jr., Howard Cournoyer, Bob Sciretta
Key Grip . . . . Rich Guinness, Jr.
Best Boy Grip . . . . Glen Engels
Dolly Grip . . . . Pat McGrath
Grips . . . . Howard Davidson, Victor Huey,
Wesley Battle, Paul Volo, Kevin Lowry,
Kevin Gilligan, Charlie Price
Key Rigging Grip . . . . . . Billy Kerwick
Rigging Best Boy Grip . . . . Joseph Viano
Rigging Grips . . . . . John Bolz, Thomas
Yostpille, Rory Walsh, Tommy Ryan, Gerard
Lowry, Richie Montgomery, Chris Primavera
Special Effects Supervisor . . . Steve Kirshoff
Special Effects Coordinator . . John Stifanich
Special Effects Foreman . . . . Robert Scupp
Assistant Costume Designer
. . . . Michelle Matland
Costume Design Assistants . Mitchell Bloom
Patrick Wiley
Costume Supervisors . . . . Donna Maloney
Kate Edwards
Costume Assistant . . . . Jonathan Schwartz
Costume Coordinator . . . . Melissa Haley
Costume Shop Supervisors . . . Patty Eiben
Amy Andrews
Head Seamstress/Tailor . . . Laurie Buehler
Seamstress/Tailor . . . . . Celeste Livingston
Seamstress . . . . Elizabeth Muxi
Set Costumer . . . . Ben Wilson
Costumer . . . . Bryan Matheson

Costumer to Mr. Damon . . . Barnaby Smith
Costumer to Ms. Jolie . . . . . . Iris Lemos
Makeup Department Head/Designer
. . . . Carla White
Key Makeup/Co-Designer . . Todd Kleitsch
Assistant Makeup . . . . Rita Ogden
Hairstyles by . . . . Alan Dangerio
Hair Co-Department Head . . Jerry Popolis
Assistant Hair . . . . John Quaglia
Makeup Artist to Mr. Damon
. . . . Chrissie Beveridge
Makeup Artist to Ms. Jolie . Toni Garavaglia
Hair Stylist to Mr. Damon . . Kay Georgiou
Hair Stylist to Ms. Jolie . . . . Colin Jamison
Script Supervisor . . . . Eva Cabrera
Location Manager . . . . . Christie Mullen
Assistant Location Managers
. . . . Lynn H. Powers
Eric Wrolstad
Second Assistant Location Managers
. . . . Elizabeth Klenk
Joe Stephans
Location Coordinators . . . . Dave Ferguson
. . . . Phuong-Thuy Pham
Second Unit Director . . . . . Rob Legato
Second Unit Assistant Director . . Ron Ames
First Assistant Editor . . . . . Adam Geiger
Editorial Production Assistant
. . . . Carlos Mare Rodriguez
Post Production Assistant . . . . Nick Olson
Supervising Sound Editor / Sound Designer
. . . . Warren Shaw
Supervising Dialogue / ADR Editor
. . . . Tony Martinez
First Assistant Sound Editor
. . . . Steve Schwartz
Dialogue Editors . . . . . . Laura Civiello,
John Werner, Dan Korintus
ADR Editors . . . . Jane McCulley
Kenton Jakub
Sound Effects Editor . . . . Jacob Ribicoff
Foley Editors . . . William Sweeney, Eytan
Mirsky, Stuart Stanley, Bruce Kitzmeyer
Assistant Sound Editor . . . . . Eric Strausser
Apprentice Sound Editor . . . . Allen Lau
Re-Recordist . . . . Harry Higgins
Mix Assistant . . . . Martin Czembor
Foley Mixer . . . . George Lara
Foley Artist . . . . Marko Costanzo
Sound Effects Recordist . . . Coll Anderson
ADR Mixers . . . . David Boulton, Weldon
Brown, Bobby Johanson, Ron Bedrosian,
Doug Murray, Nick Kray, Michael Miller,
Wendy Czajkowsky

159

ADR Voice Casting
. . . . . . Dann Fink/Loopers Unlimited
Re-Recording Mixers. . . Reilly Steele, Lee
    Dichter, Warren Shaw, Martin Czembor
Mix Technicians . . . . Bob Troeller
    Avi Laniado
Sound Re-Recordist . . . . . Harry Higgins
Re-Recording Services by
. . . . Sound One Corp.
Supervising Music Editors
. . . . E. Gedney Webb
Music Editor. . . . . . . Shari L. Johanson
Score Recorded and Mixed at
. . . . Legacy Studios, New York
Score Recorded and Mixed by
. . . . Lawrence Manchester
Score Recorded by . . . . . Richard King
    Josiah Gluck
Orchestration. . . . . . Sonny Kompanek,
    Walt Fowler, Rick Giovinazzo, Ladd
    McIntosh, Bruce Fowler
Conducted by . . . . . . Jonathan Scheffer
Digital Recordists . . . . Brian Pugh
    Tim Starnes
Digital Orchestral Timings . . . Nancy Allen
Music Preparation . . . . Tony Finno
    Booker White
Music Contractor . . . . Sandra Park
Composer Technical Support . Dean Parker,
    Mark Baechle, Daniel Levy
Visual Effects Producer. . . . . Ron Ames
Visual Effects Coordinator. . . Adam Gerstel
Visual Effects by theBasement
    Brian Battles
    Stephen Lawes

Visual Effects by CafeFX Inc.
Visual Effects Supervisor . . . . David Ebner
Visual Effects Producer . Richard Ivan Mann
VFX Coordinators. . . . . . Wendy Hulbert
    Dawn Turner
FX Animators . . . . Will Nicholson
    Phil Giles
Compositors. . . . . Edwardo Mendez
    Richard R. Reed
    Michael Kennen
Managing Editor . . . . . . Desi R. Ortiz
VFX Editor . . . . . Bernardo Rodriguez
3D Matchmover . . . . Kevin Hoppe
Rotoscope/2D Paint Artists
. . . . Lindsay M. Anderson
    Ruben Rodas
    Toby Newell
3-D Technical Support. . . Brian Openshaw

Production Executives . . . Jeffrey T. Barnes
    O.D. Welch
Executive Producer
. . . . Vicki Galloway Weimer
Business Development. . . . Steve Dellerson
Digital Backlot
Robert Stromberg
Paul Graff
Visual Effects & Animation by New Deal
Studios, Inc.
Visual Effects Supervisor. . Matthew Gratzner
Digital Supervisor . . . . . Anthony Riazzi
Producer . . . . David Sanger
Miniature Effects Crew Chief
. . . . Forest P. Fischer
Model Makers . . . . . . Enrico Altmann,
Seth Curlin, Adam Gelbart, Raymond Moore
Lead Painter . . . . . Leigh-Alexandra Jacob
First Assistant Camera. . . . . A.J. Raitano
MoCo Camera Operator . . Joshua Cushner
Coordinator . . . . E. M. Bowen
Compositors . . Jeffrey Jasper, Jeffrey Kalmus,
    Ned Wilson
Production Controller . . . . . Frank Ellison
Production Accountant . . Lynda Van Damm
First Assistant Accountant . . . . Amy Carter
Second Assistant Accountants
. . . . Rebecca Glew
    John Whitley
Payroll Accountants . . . . . Sally Douglass
    Sarah Rubenstein
Accounting Clerks. . . . . Rachel Gonzales,
    Chris Camuto, Leah Deveau, Minico
    Roberts, Jennifer Markowitz

Production Coordinator . . Rhonda George
Assistant Production Coordinator
. . . . Leda Nornang
Travel Coordinator . . . . Meghan Wicker
Production Secretaries . . . Ulises Rodriguez
    Richard P. Keeshan
Assistants to Mr. De Niro . . Ryan McCormick,
    Amy L. Weinblum, Sheenagh O'Rourke
Assistants to Mr. J.G. Robinson . . Janet West
Assistant to Ms. Rosenthal . . Meghan Lyvers
Assistant to Mr. Damon . . . Colin J. O'Hara
Assistant to Ms. Jolie . . . . . Holly Goline
Assistant to Mr. Brigham . . . Rita Colimon
Second Second Assistant Director
. . . . Kali Harrison
DGA Trainee. . . . . Marissa Kaplan
Location Assistants . . . Derek J. Manganelli,
    Joshua Shull, Paul Lucero, Vincent Taylor,
    Colby Shrefler, Michael Uribe, Bill Bahen

160

Office Production Assistants . . . . . Steven Spencer, Robert Ford, Michele Nieves

Art Department Production Assistants . . . . Bradley Weinrieb, Josephine Shokrian, Katie Stern

Set Dec Production Assistants . . . . Elizabeth Jane Franz Jennifer Massi

Set Production Assistants . . . . . Bill Ahern, Mirashyam Blakeslee, Thomas K. Lee, Tal Perry, Ben Ruggiero, Nate Grubb, Natalie Brown, Ani Williams

Costume Production Assistants . . . . Emily Gunshor, Katie Chihaby, Megan Asbee

Construction Production Assistants . . . . Jonathan Bernier, Lawrence Watford, Giuseppe Centola

Parking Coordinator . . . . Leo Driver

Security . . . . MSL Security

Casting Associate . . . . Kate Bulpitt

Casting Assistant . . . . . . Samantha Finkler

Extras Casting . . . . . Grant Wilfley Casting

Extras Casting Associates . . . . Heather Reidenbach Ingrid Jungermann

Theatrical Staging Supervisor . . . . David Chambers

Technical Advisor . . . . Jon Monett

Unit Publicist . . . . Julie Kuehndorf

Still Photographer . . . . . Andy Schwartz

Research Advisor . . . . Jason Sosnoff

Legal Liaison . . . . Kaisa Akerlund

Script Clearances . . . . . . Ashley Kravitz

Product Placement Coordinator . . . . Betina O'Mara

Stock Footage Researcher . . . . Christina Lowery

Dialect Coaches . . . . Tim Monich Howard Samuelson

On-Set Medic . . . . . . Maureen Beitler

Choreographer . . . . Julie Arenal

Assistant Choreographer . . . . Wesley Fata

Theatrical Staging Assistant . . . . Kara-Lynn Vaeni

Etiquette Coach . . . . Lily Lodge

Construction Coordinator . . . . Kenneth D. Nelson

Shop Craft Foreman . . . . James Sadek

Key Construction Grip . . . . . Peter Betulia

Shop Electric . . . . . Peter John Petraglia

Construction Foremen . . . . John Johnston Robert Dillon

Best Boy Construction Grip . . Klaus Schreiber

Lead Greensman . . . . . . Mark Selemon

Charge Scenic . . . . Roland Brooks

Scenic Foreman . . . . John Ralbovsky

Scenic Gang Boss . . . . Giovanni Rodriguez

Transportation Captain . . . . James Fanning

Transportation Co-Captain . . Eddie Fanning

Catering . . . . Hanna Brothers Coast-to-Coast

Craft Service . . . . . McKenna Bros, Terry Levenberg, Mike McKenna, Steven Wargo, Kendra Levenberg

Dominican Republic Unit

Production Supervisor . . . . . . Sean Fogel

Assistant Unit Production Manager . . . . Santiago Quinones

Second Assistant Directors . . . . Humberto Castellanos Ivan Herrera

Second A Camera Assistants . . . . Anthony Hechanova Fabio Iadeluca

Camera Loaders . . . . . Julian de Le Cruz Alex Scott

Sound Mixer . . . . Eric Taveras

Boom Operator . . . . . Andres Gonzalez

Art Director . . . . Miguel Lopez Castillo

Assistant Art Directors . . . Arturo Berastein Fernando Andujar

Graphic Designer . . . . Julio Castillo

Art Department Coordinator . . . . Martha Mitchell

On Set Dressers . . . . Monika Frias

Leadman . . . . Carl Catanese

Property Master . . . . . James Stubblefield

Electrics . . . . Jacinto Reyes, Jose Montero, Francisco Adames, Cristino Adames

Grip . . . . Amaury Jimenez

Special Effects . . . . Rafael Arias, Clemente Portillo, Marc Dalet

Makeup . . . . Patricia Regan Tatiana Dulovic Donna Premick

Hair . . . . Alfida Fernandez

Location Manager . . . Joaquin Diego Prange

Assistant Location Manager . . Jorge Guzman

Second Assistant Location Manager . . . . Rafael Rivera

Location Coordinator . . . . Mariana Galvez Cordero

First Assistant Accountant . . Lisa Shillingburg

Second Assistant Accountants . . Maira Suarez Catalina Lora

Payroll Accountant . . . . . Gary M. Clark

161

Accounting Clerk
. . . . Clara Dominguez De Diaz
Production Coordinator . . Ulises Rodriguez
Assistant Production Coordinator
. . . . Giselle Mangual Perez
Production Secretary . . . . Linel Hernandez
Extras Casting . . . . Tom Gustafson
Still Photographer . . . . David Lee
Construction Coordinator
. . . . Thomas A. Morris
General Foreman . . . . . Daniel Dietrich
Construction Foremen . Juan Bautista Ramos
Scenic Foreman . . . . . Alejandra Martinez
Scenic Gang Boss . . . . Guifre Tort
Transportation Coordinators . . Josivan Rojas
Ludwig Mangual
Aerial Coordinator . . . . . . Bill Richards

London Unit
Unit Production Manager . . . Rachel Neale
Second Assistant Director . . . . Phil Booth
Second A Camera Assistant . . . . Kate Filby
B Camera Operator / Steadicam
. . . . Alf Tramontin
First B Camera Assistant . . . Sam Garwood
Second B Camera Assistant
. . . . Alessandra Sangermano
Boom Operator . . . . John Casali
Sound Maintenance . . . . . . Chris Murphy
Supervising Art Director . . . . . Keith Pain
Assistant Art Directors . . . . . Harry Pain
Sloane U'Ren
Set Decorator . . . . Jille Azis
Property Master . . . . David Balfour
Chargehand Standby Props . . Bradley Torbett
Gaffer . . . . Chuck Finch
Rigging Gaffer . . . . Tommy Finch
Best Boy . . . . Billy Merrell
Grips . . . . Davie Appleby
James Crowther
Special Effects Supervisor . . . Stuart Brisdon
Technicians . . . . . . Terry Palmer, Nigel
Wilkinson, Robin Beavis
Costume Supervisor . . . . Allison Wyldeck
Makeup . . . . Marilyn MacDonald
Hair Stylist . . . . . Maureen Hetherington
Location Manager . . . . Ben Rimmer
Assistant Location Manager . . Ian Pollington
Unit Managers . . . . Terry Blyther
Production Accountant . . . . Paul Cadiou
Production Coordinator
. . . . Francesca Castellano
Assistant Production Coordinator
. . . . Holly Pullinger

Third Assistant Director . . . . Vicky Marks
UK Casting . . . . Sue Jones
Construction Coordinator . . . Gene D'Cruz
Transportation Coordinator
. . . . Gary Birmingham

Washington, DC Unit
Production Supervisor . . . . . . Sean Fogel
Second Assistant Director
. . . . Ruben Flores Rios II
Location Manager . . . . . . John Latenser
Location Coordinator . . . . . Carol Flaisher
Transportation Coordinator . . Gilbert Young

"H.M.S. PINAFORE: ACT 1: HAIL! MEN
O'WAR'S MEN...I'M CALLED LITTLE
BUTTERCUP"
Performed by Matt Damon and Cast

"THE WHIFFENPOOF SONG (BAA!
BAA! BAA!)"
Written by George S. Pomeroy, Meade
Minnegerode, Tod B. Galloway
Rev. by Rudy Vallee,
Special lyrics by Moss Hart

"FOOLS RUSH IN"
Written by Rube Bloom, Johnny Mercer
Produced by Bruce Fowler
Performed by Vince Giordano and The
Nighthawks Orchestra

"TRIBECA BOUNCE"
Written and Produced by Bruce Fowler
Performed by Vince Giordano and The
Nighthawks Orchestra

"NO RAIN A FALLIN"
Written and Produced by Bruce Fowler
Performed by Vince Giordano and The
Nighthawks Orchestra

"SALVE REGINA"
Written and Performed by Arvo Part
Courtesy of Hyperion Records Limited

"So in Love"
Written by Bruce Fowler, Harry Garfield
Produced by Bruce Fowler
Performed by Vince Giordano and The
Nighthawks Orchestra

"I'll Always Remember"
Written and Produced by Bruce Fowler
Performed by Vince Giordano and The
Nighthawks Orchestra

"LITANY"
Written by Arvo Part
Performed by The Hilliard Ensemble, The
Tallinn Chamber Orchestra, and the Estonian
Philharmonic Chamber Choir, Tõnu
Kaljuste, conductor
Courtesy of ECM Records

"BLUE SKIES"
Written by Irving Berlin

"EMBRACEABLE YOU"
Written by George Gershwin, Ira Gershwin

"NIGHT AND DAY"
Written by Cole Porter

"WHERE OR WHEN"
Written by Lorenz Hart and Richard Rodgers
Produced by Bruce Fowler
Performed by Vince Giordano and The
Nighthawks Orchestra

"O CHRISTMAS TREE"
Performed by The Brentwood Singers
Courtesy of Brentwood Records/Provident
Label Group

"THERE IS NOTHIN' LIKE A DAME"
Written by Richard Rodgers, Oscar
Hammerstein II

"LET THE SUN SHINE FOREVER"
Written by Lev Oshanin, Avraam Ilich
Ostrovskij
Performed by Mark Ivanir

"OFRENDA DE AMOR"
Performed by St. Louis African Chorus
Recorded At Sheldon Concert Hall, St.
Louis, MO

"H.M.S. PINAFORE: ACT 1: HAIL! MEN
O'WAR'S MEN ... I'M CALLED LITTLE
BUTTERCUP"
Performed by The D'Oyly Carte Opera
Company, Gillian Knight And The New
Symphony Orchestra Of London Conductor
Isidore Godfrey
Courtesy Of Decca Music Group Limited
Under License From Universal Music
Enterprises

"COME RAIN OR COME SHINE"
Written by Harold Arlen, Johnny Mercer

"SILOUANS SONG"
Written by Arvo Part
Performed by The Tallinn Chamber
Orchestra
Courtesy of ECM Records

PLAYBACK & STOCK FOOTAGE
PROVIDED BY
Archive Films by Getty Images
BBC
British Film Institute
ITN Source/Fox Movietonenews, Inc.
John F. Kennedy Library Foundation
Producers Library
Stock footage courtesy The WPA
Film Library

Title Design . . . . theBasement
Stephen Lawes
Negative Cutter
. . . . Buena Vista Negative Cutting
Chapman Camera Dollies . . Paskal Lighting
Color Timer . . . . Terry Haggar
Digital Intermediate by
. . . . . Technicolor Digital Intermediates
Digital Film Colorist. . . Stephen Nakamura
Digital Intermediate Producer
. . . . Gregg Schaublin
Optical Sound Negative by . . . . NT Audio
Dolby Sound Consultant. . Steve F. B. Smith
Camera Equipment by . . . . . . Panavision
Lighting Equipment by . . . Paskal Lighting
Grip Equipment by
. . . . K & G Grip Equipment
Stage Rigging Equipment by
. . . . See Factor Industries, Inc.
Editing Equipment provided by
. . . . Electric Picture Solutions
Digital Dailies Provided by . . Complete Post
Digital Dailies Colorist. . . . . . . Sparkle
Digital Dailies Project Manager . Kevin Buck
Production Financing provided by
. . . . Citibank (West)
FSB
U.S. Bank National Association
Insurance provided by
. AON Albert G. Ruben Insurance Services
Completion Guaranty provided by
. . . . International Film Guarantors

163

The Producers would like to thank the following for their help and cooperation in the making of this film:

Aerodom
Amet
Bureau of Engraving and Printing
The Dominican Armed Forces
Dominican Film Commission
The Dominican Republic Ministry of Culture
The Dominican Republic Ministry of Customs
Peter Kornbluh
Keith Melton
The NYPD Movie and Television Unit
The NYC Mayor's Office of Film, Theater and Broadcasting, Commissioner Katherine L. Oliver
New York State Governor's Office for Motion Picture and Television Development, Pat Swinney Kaufman, Executive Director
State of New York Division of Military & Naval Affairs, Bedford Avenue Armory, Grace Clark, Superintendent
Residents of Capitol Hill
United States Department of Agriculture
United States National Park Service - National Capital Region
United States Park Police
United States Senate
Washington Metropolitan Area Transit Authority (WMATA)
The Willard Intercontinental Hotel

MPAA #43094

ABOUT THE FILMMAKERS

Academy Award® recipient **ERIC ROTH** (Written by) attended the University of California at Santa Barbara, Columbia University and UCLA. He won the Samuel Goldwyn Writing Award while attending UCLA.

His first produced screenplay was *The Nickel Ride* in 1975, directed by Robert Mulligan, which premiered at the Cannes Film Festival. Some of the movies Roth has written include *Suspect*, with Cher and Dennis Quaid; *Mr. Jones*, with Richard Gere and directed by Mike Figgis; *Forrest Gump*, for which he won an Academy Award® and the Writers Guild Award for Best Adapted Screenplay; *The Horse Whisperer*, directed by Robert Redford; *The Insider*, directed by Michael Mann and starring Al Pacino and Russell Crowe, for which he was nominated for an Academy Award® and Writers Guild Award and won the Humanitas Award. Roth also wrote *Ali*, directed by Michael Mann and starring Will Smith. Most recently, Roth co-wrote the 2005 Academy Award®-nominated screenplay *Munich*, directed by Steven Spielberg.

Roth's current motion pictures include *Lucky You*, directed by Curtis Hanson and starring Eric Bana, Drew Barrymore and Robert Duvall. He has recently written *The Curious Case of Benjamin Button*—directed by David Fincher, produced by Kathleen Kennedy and starring Brad Pitt and Cate Blanchett—which is currently filming in New Orleans. Roth has also completed the screenplay *Shantaram*, an upcoming film starring Johnny Depp.

ROBERT DE NIRO (Directed by/Produced by/General Sullivan) launched his prolific motion picture career in Brian De Palma's *The Wedding Party* in 1969. By 1973, De Niro twice won the New York Film Critics Award for Best Supporting Actor in recognition of his critically acclaimed performances in *Bang the Drum Slowly* and Martin Scorsese's *Mean Streets*.

In 1974, De Niro received the Academy Award® for Best Supporting Actor for his portrayal of the young Vito Corleone in *The Godfather: Part II*. In 1980, he won his second Oscar®, this time for Best Actor, for his extraordinary portrayal of Jake La Motta in Scorsese's *Raging Bull*. De Niro has earned Academy Award® nominations in four additional films: as Travis Bickle in Scorsese's acclaimed *Taxi Driver*, as a Vietnam vet in Michael Cimino's *The Deer Hunter*, as a catatonic patient brought to life in Penny Marshall's *Awakenings* and in 1992 as Max Cady, an ex-con looking for revenge in Scorsese's remake of the 1962 classic *Cape Fear*.

De Niro's distinguished body of work also includes performances in Elia Kazan's *The Last Tycoon*; Bernardo Bertolucci's *1900*; Ulu Grosbard's *True Confessions* and *Falling in Love*; Sergio Leone's *Once Upon a Time in America*;

Scorsese's *The King of Comedy*, *New York, New York*, *Goodfellas* and *Casino*; Terry Gilliam's *Brazil*; Roland Joffé's *The Mission*; Brian De Palma's *The Untouchables*; Alan Parker's *Angel Heart*; Martin Brest's *Midnight Run*; David Hugh Jones' *Jacknife*; Martin Ritt's *Stanley & Iris*; Neil Jordan's *We're No Angels*; Ron Howard's *Backdraft*; Michael Caton-Jones' *This Boy's Life*; John McNaughton's *Mad Dog and Glory*; *A Bronx Tale*; Kenneth Branagh's *Mary Shelley's Frankenstein*; Michael Mann's *Heat*; Barry Levinson's *Sleepers* and *Wag the Dog*; Jerry Zaks' *Marvin's Room*; Tony Scott's *The Fan*; James Mangold's *Cop Land*; Alfonso Cuarón's *Great Expectations*; Quentin Tarantino's *Jackie Brown*; John Frankenheimer's *Ronin*; Harold Ramis' *Analyze This* and *Analyze That*; Joel Schumacher's *Flawless*; Des McAnuff's *The Adventures of Rocky and Bullwinkle*; Jay Roach's *Meet the Parents*; George Tillman, Jr.'s *Men of Honor*; John Herzfeld's *15 Minutes*; Frank Oz's *The Score*; Tom Dey's *Showtime*; Michael Caton-Jones' *City by the Sea*; and Nick Hamm's *Godsend*. His most recent works are John Polson's *Hide and Seek*, the animated film *Shark Tale*, and Roach's *Meet the Fockers*. Next, De Niro will star in *Stardust*, with Michelle Pfeiffer, Claire Danes and Sienna Miller, and directed by Matthew Vaughn.

De Niro takes pride in the development of his production company, Tribeca Productions, and the Tribeca Film Center, which he founded with Jane Rosenthal in 1988. Through Tribeca, he develops projects on which he serves in a combination of capacities, including producer, director and actor.

Tribeca's *A Bronx Tale* marked De Niro's directorial debut. Other Tribeca features include *Thunderheart*, *Cape Fear*, *Mistress*, *Night and the City*, *The Night We Never Met*, *Faithful*, *Panther*, *Marvin's Room*, *Wag the Dog*, *Analyze This*, *Flawless*, *The Adventures of Rocky and Bullwinkle*, *Meet the Parents*, *15 Minutes*, *Showtime*, *Analyze That* and *Meet the Fockers*. In 1992, Tribeca TV was launched with the critically acclaimed series *Tribeca*. De Niro served as one of the series' executive producers.

In 1998, Tribeca produced a miniseries for NBC, *Witness to the Mob*, based on the life of Sammy "The Bull" Gravano.

In 2002, De Niro, Rosenthal and Craig Hatkoff created The Tribeca Film Festival, founded to foster the economic and cultural revitalization of Lower Manhattan through an annual celebration of film, music and culture. The Festival's mission is to promote New York City as a major filmmaking center and to help filmmakers reach the broadest possible audience. Since its inception, the Tribeca Film Festival has found critical and popular success. Reflecting the Festival's continued growth, it expanded in 2006 to more neighborhoods throughout Manhattan and feature screenings, special events, concerts, a family street fair and panel discussions.

Tribeca Productions is headquartered at De Niro's Tribeca Film Center, in the TriBeCa district of New York.